INDIANA JONES
ADVENTURES

NEW YORK

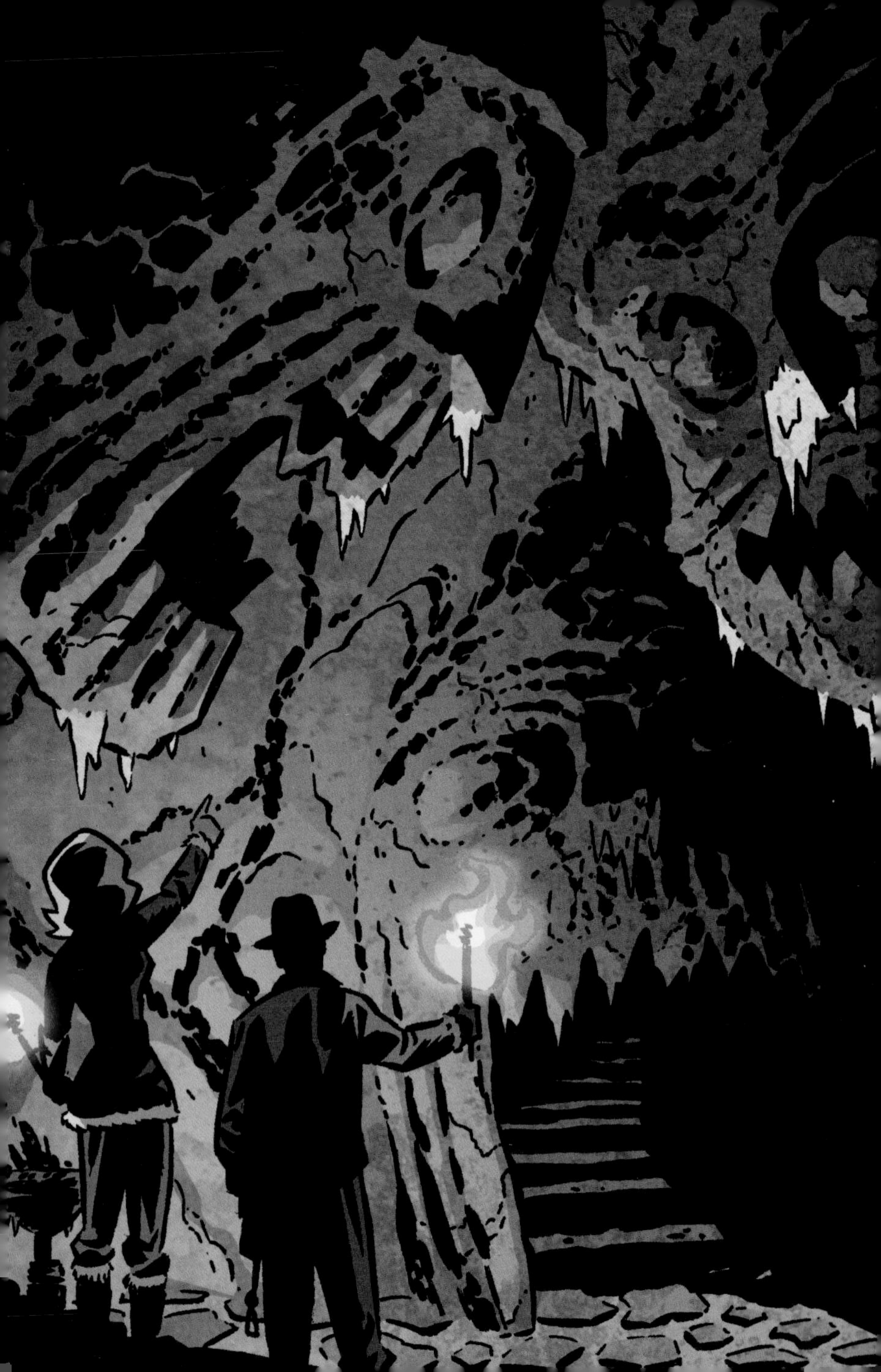

INDIANA JONES™ ADVENTURES VOL 1

Script
Philip Gelatt

Art
Ethen Beavers

Colors
Ronda Pattison

Letters
Michael Heisler

Cover
Ethen Beavers
and **Ronda Pattison**

Dark Horse Books®

Publisher
Mike Richardson

Art Director
Lia Ribacchi

Collection Designer
Stephen Reichert

Assistant Editor
Patrick Thorpe

Associate Editor
Katie Moody

Editor
Dave Land

Special thanks to Elaine Mederer, Jann Moorhead, David Anderman,
Leland Chee, Frank Parisi, and Carol Roeder at Lucas Licensing

INDIANA JONES ADVENTURES VOLUME 1

Indiana Jones™ & © 2008 Lucasfilm Ltd. All rights reserved. Used under authorization.
Text and illustrations for Indiana Jones Adventures are © 2008 Lucasfilm Ltd. Dark Horse
Books® and the Dark Horse logo are registered trademarks of Dark Horse Comics, Inc. All
rights reserved. No portion of this publication may be reproduced or transmitted, in any
form or by any means, without the express written permission of Dark Horse Comics, Inc.
Names, characters, places, and incidents featured in this publication either are the product
of the author's imagination or are used fictitiously. Any resemblance to actual persons
(living or dead), events, institutions, or locales, without satiric intent, is coincidental.

Published by
Dark Horse Books
A division of Dark Horse Comics, Inc.
10956 SE Main Street
Milwaukie, OR 97222

darkhorse.com
indianajones.com

To find a comics shop in your area, call the Comic
Shop Locator Service toll-free at 1-888-266-4226

First edition: June 2008
ISBN 978-1-59307-905-5

1 3 5 7 9 10 8 6 4 2

Printed in United States of America

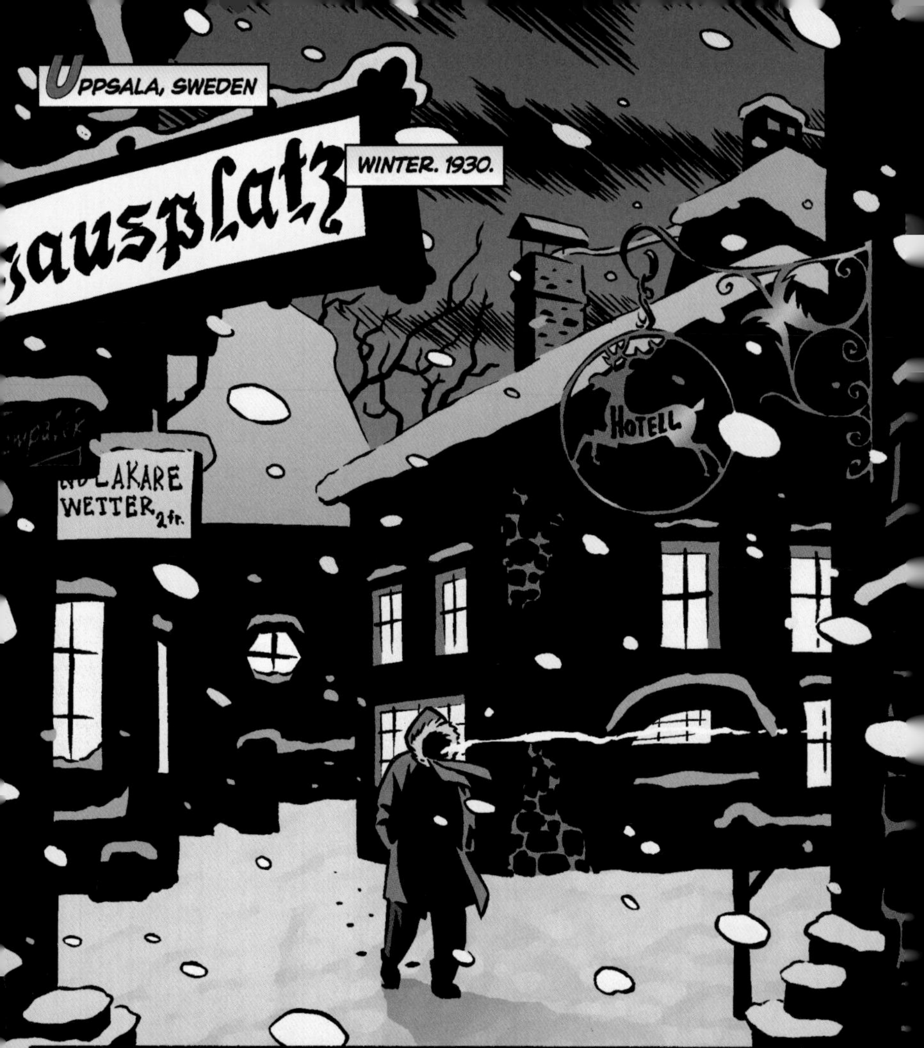
UPPSALA, SWEDEN
WINTER. 1930.
ausplatz
LAKARE
WETTER 2 fr.
HOTELL

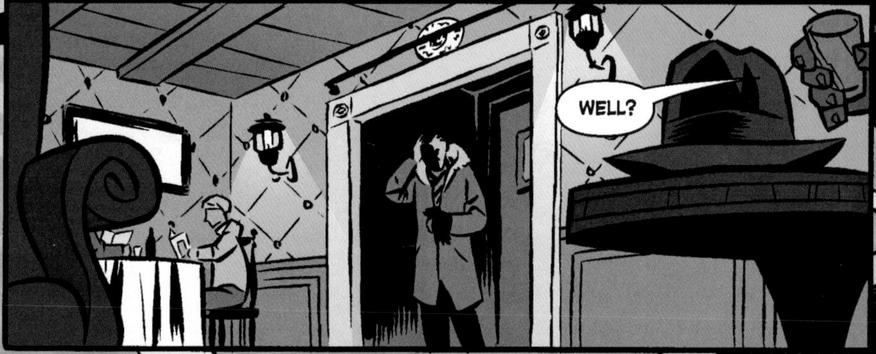
WELL?

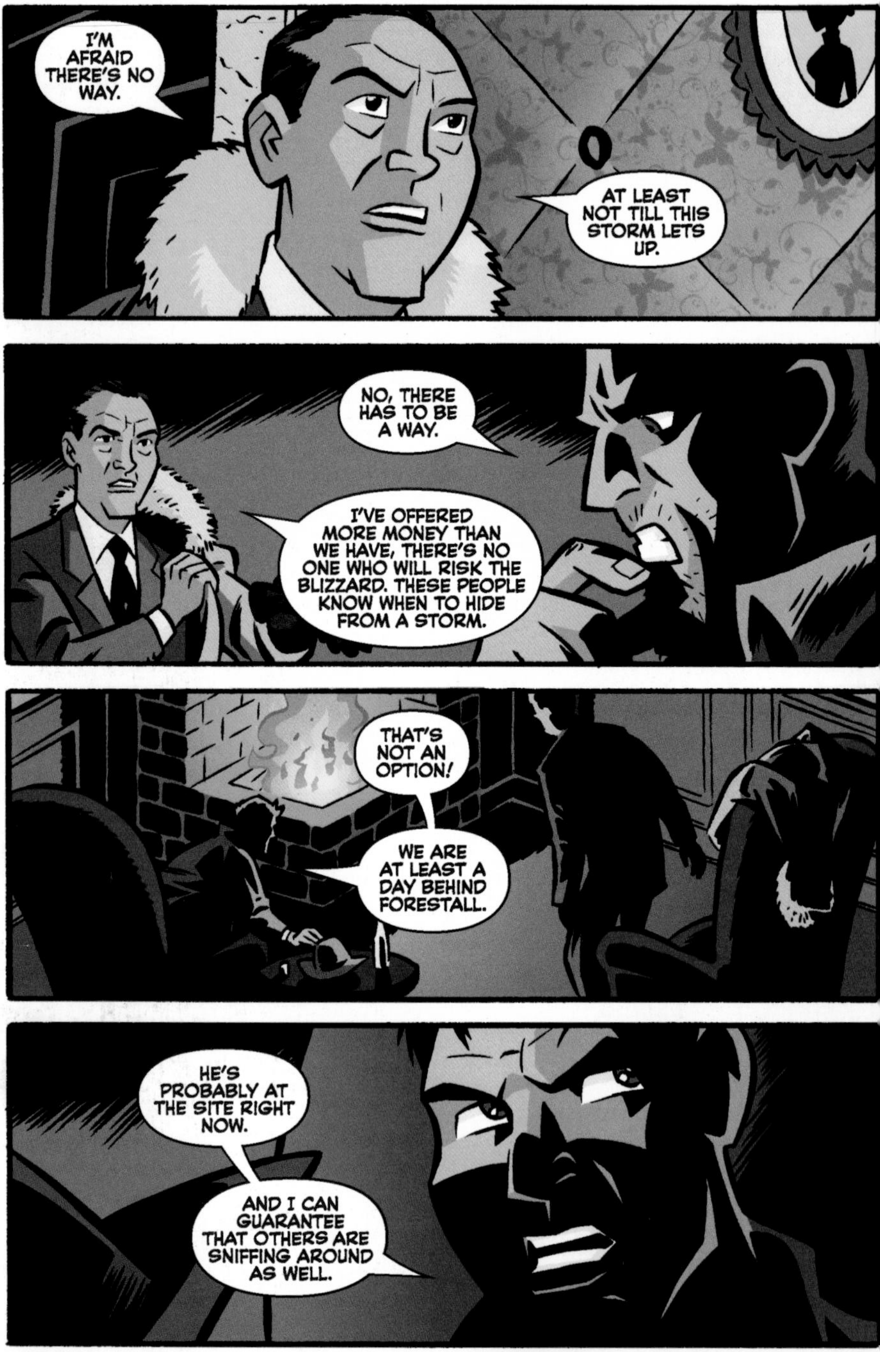
I'M AFRAID THERE'S NO WAY.
AT LEAST NOT TILL THIS STORM LETS UP.
NO, THERE HAS TO BE A WAY.
I'VE OFFERED MORE MONEY THAN WE HAVE, THERE'S NO ONE WHO WILL RISK THE BLIZZARD. THESE PEOPLE KNOW WHEN TO HIDE FROM A STORM.
THAT'S NOT AN OPTION!
WE ARE AT LEAST A DAY BEHIND FORESTALL.
HE'S PROBABLY AT THE SITE RIGHT NOW.
AND I CAN GUARANTEE THAT OTHERS ARE SNIFFING AROUND AS WELL.

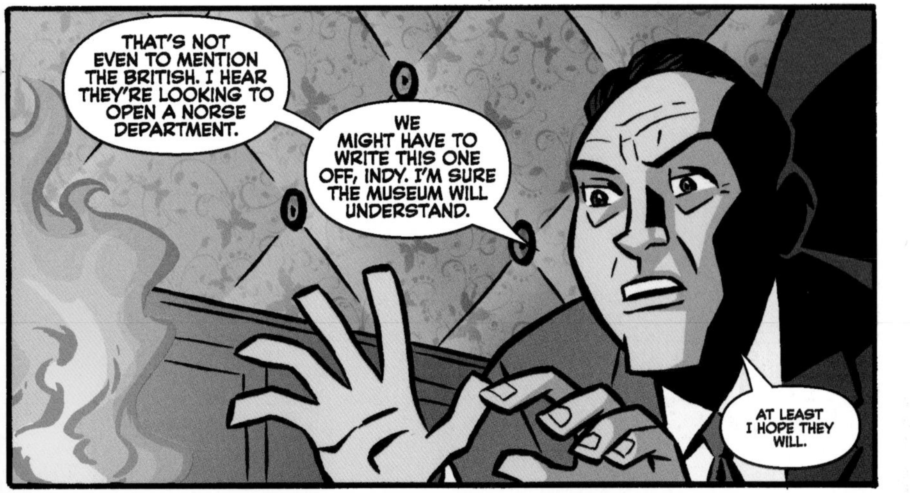
THAT'S NOT EVEN TO MENTION THE BRITISH. I HEAR THEY'RE LOOKING TO OPEN A NORSE DEPARTMENT.
WE MIGHT HAVE TO WRITE THIS ONE OFF, INDY. I'M SURE THE MUSEUM WILL UNDERSTAND.
AT LEAST I HOPE THEY WILL.

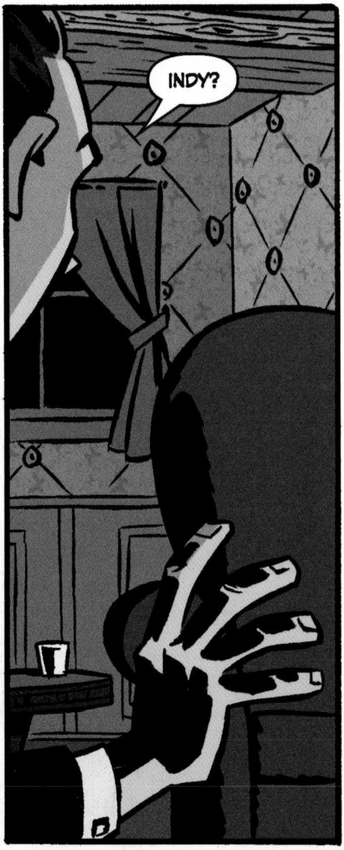
INDY?

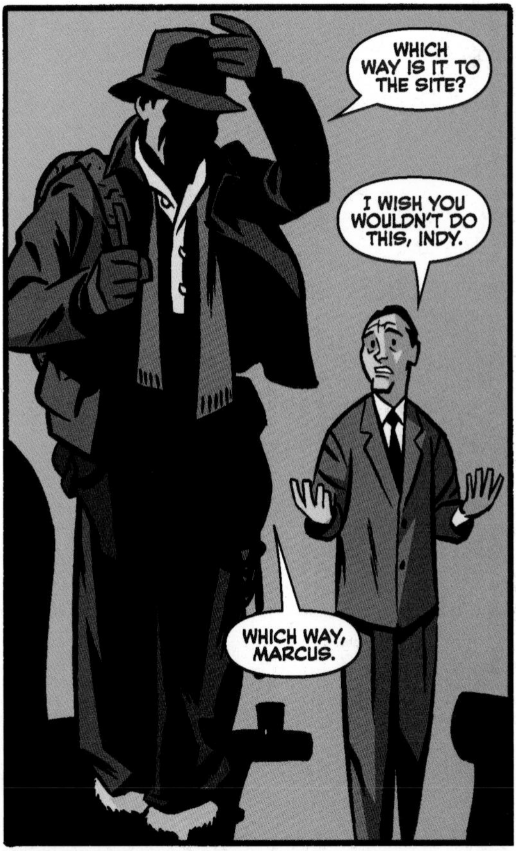
WHICH WAY IS IT TO THE SITE?
I WISH YOU WOULDN'T DO THIS, INDY.
WHICH WAY, MARCUS.

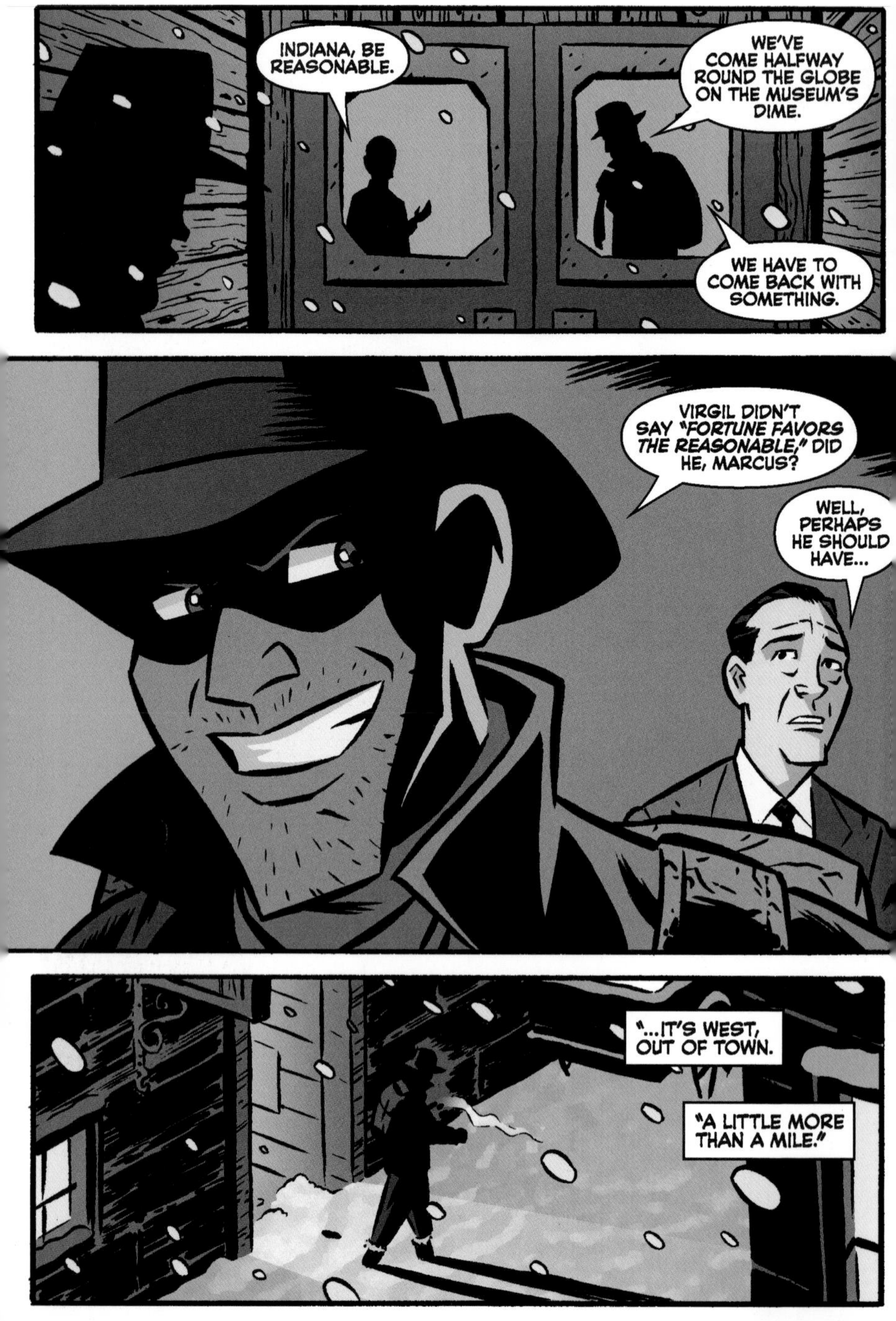
INDIANA, BE REASONABLE.
WE'VE COME HALFWAY ROUND THE GLOBE ON THE MUSEUM'S DIME.
WE HAVE TO COME BACK WITH SOMETHING.
VIRGIL DIDN'T SAY "FORTUNE FAVORS THE REASONABLE," DID HE, MARCUS?
WELL, PERHAPS HE SHOULD HAVE...
"...IT'S WEST, OUT OF TOWN.
"A LITTLE MORE THAN A MILE."

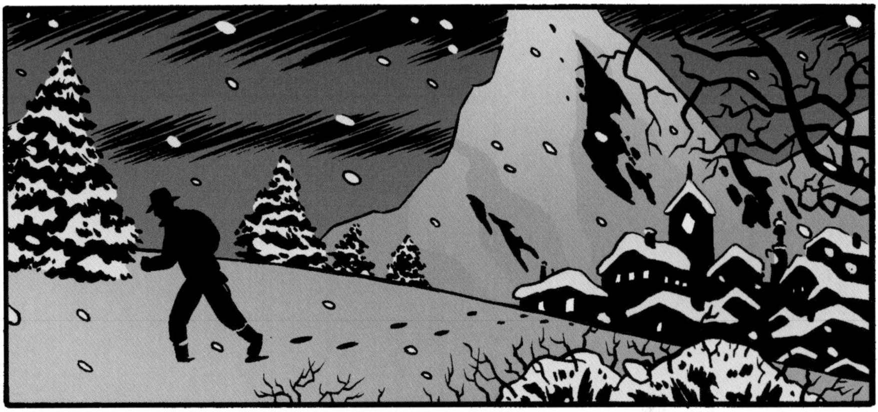
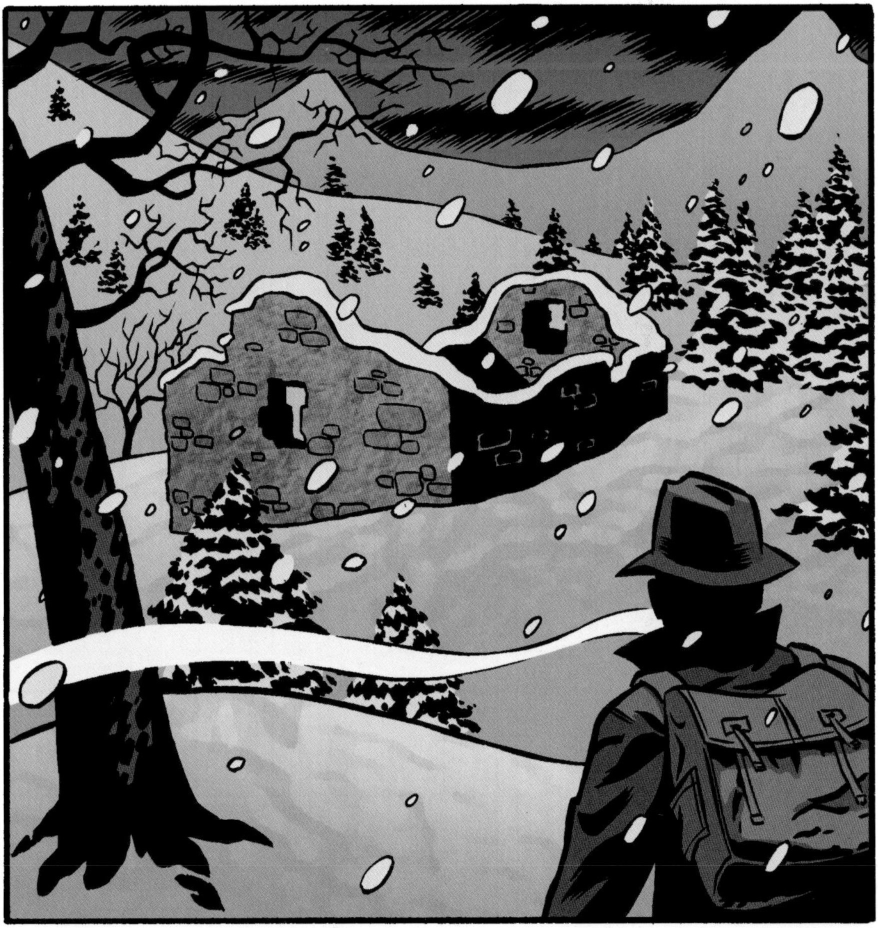

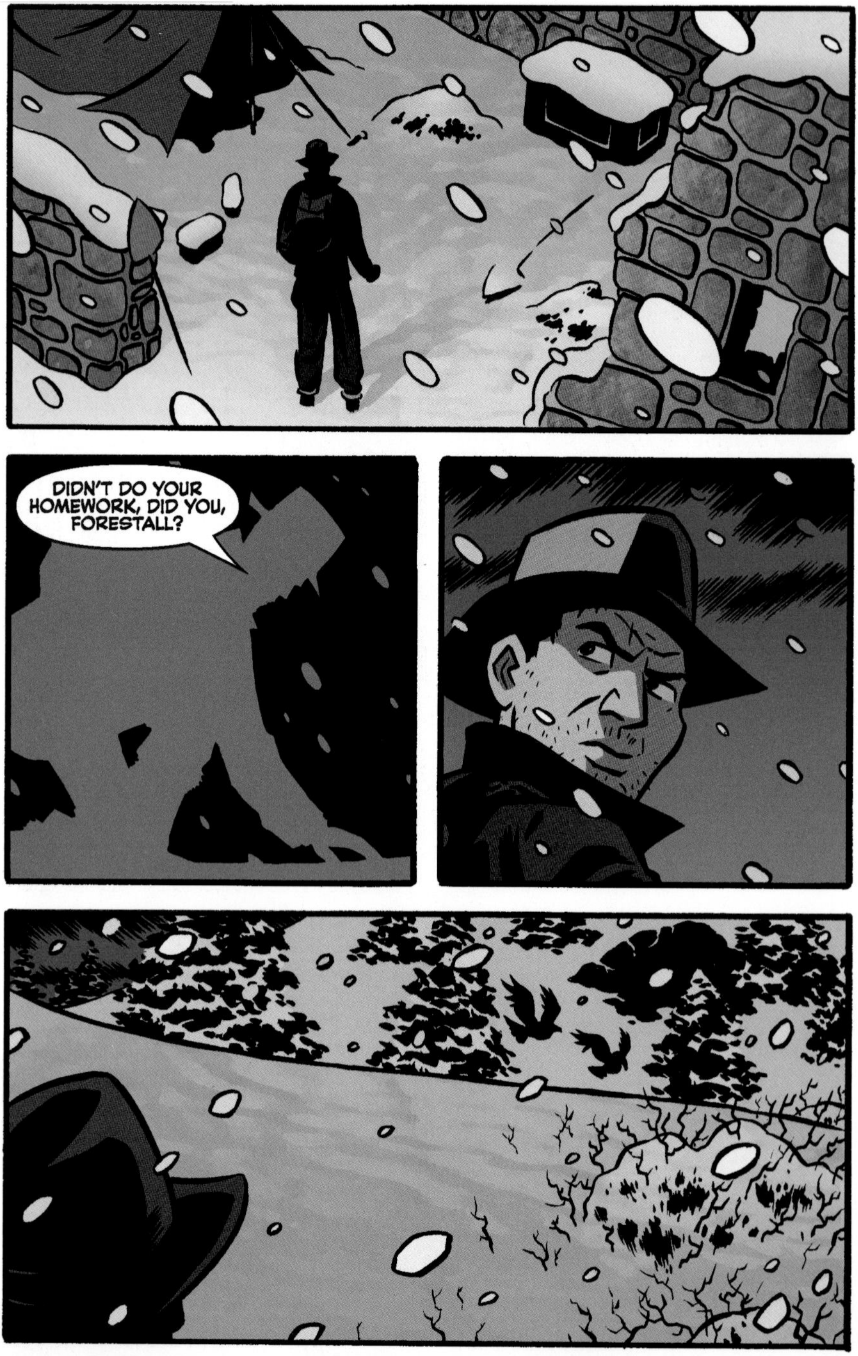
DIDN'T DO YOUR HOMEWORK, DID YOU, FORESTALL?

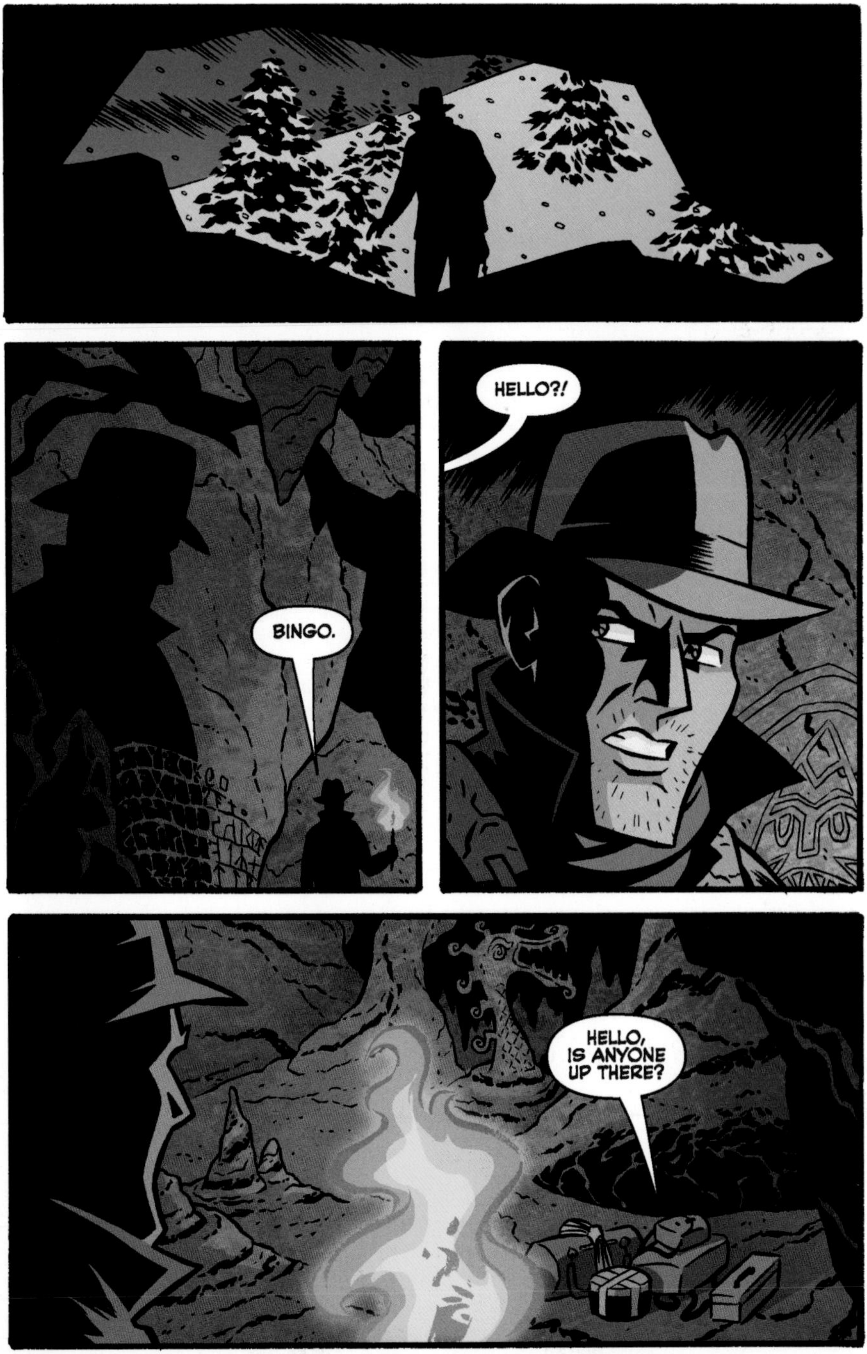
BINGO.
HELLO?!
HELLO, IS ANYONE UP THERE?

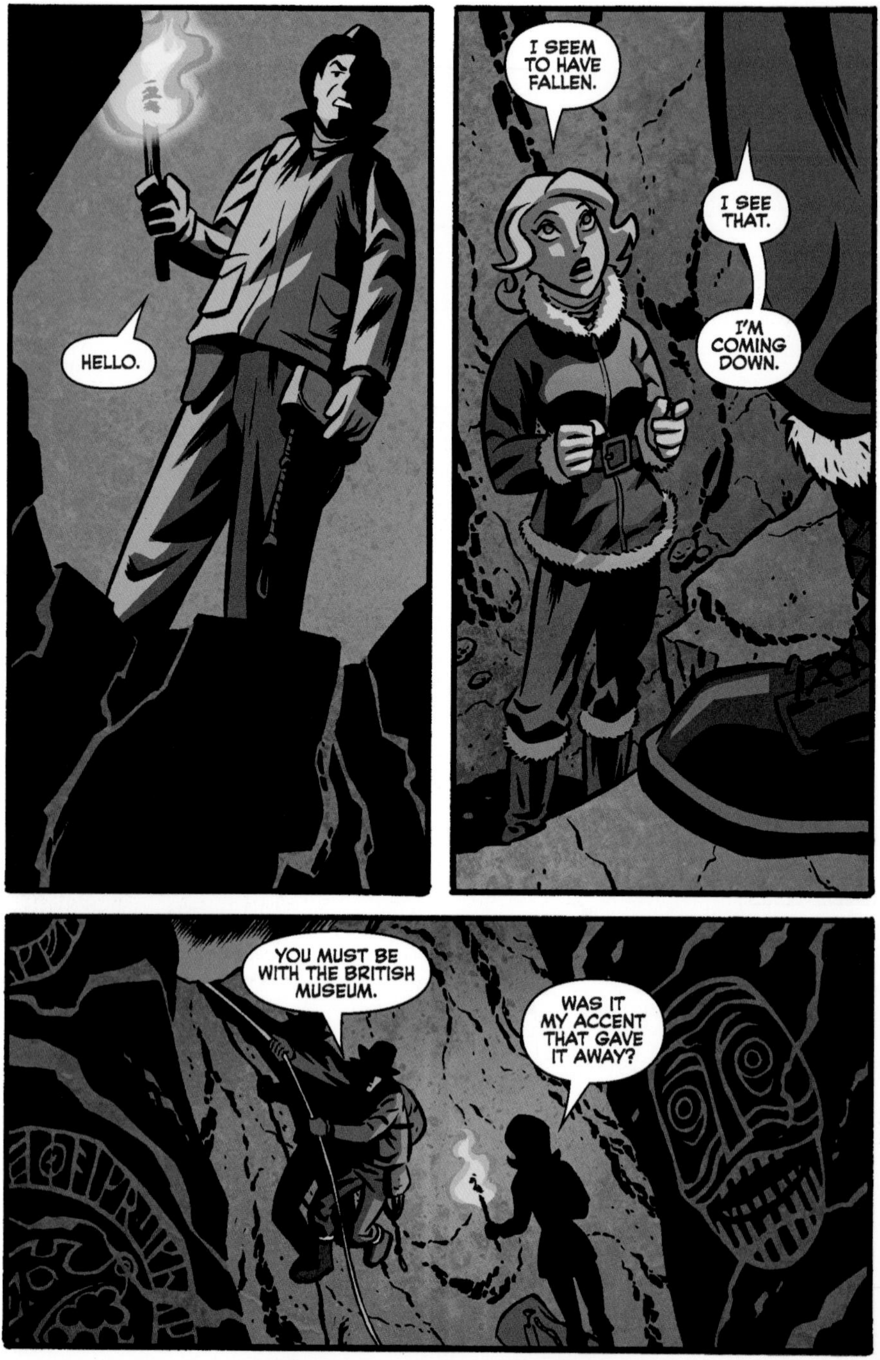
HELLO.
I SEEM TO HAVE FALLEN.
I SEE THAT.
I'M COMING DOWN.
YOU MUST BE WITH THE BRITISH MUSEUM.
WAS IT MY ACCENT THAT GAVE IT AWAY?

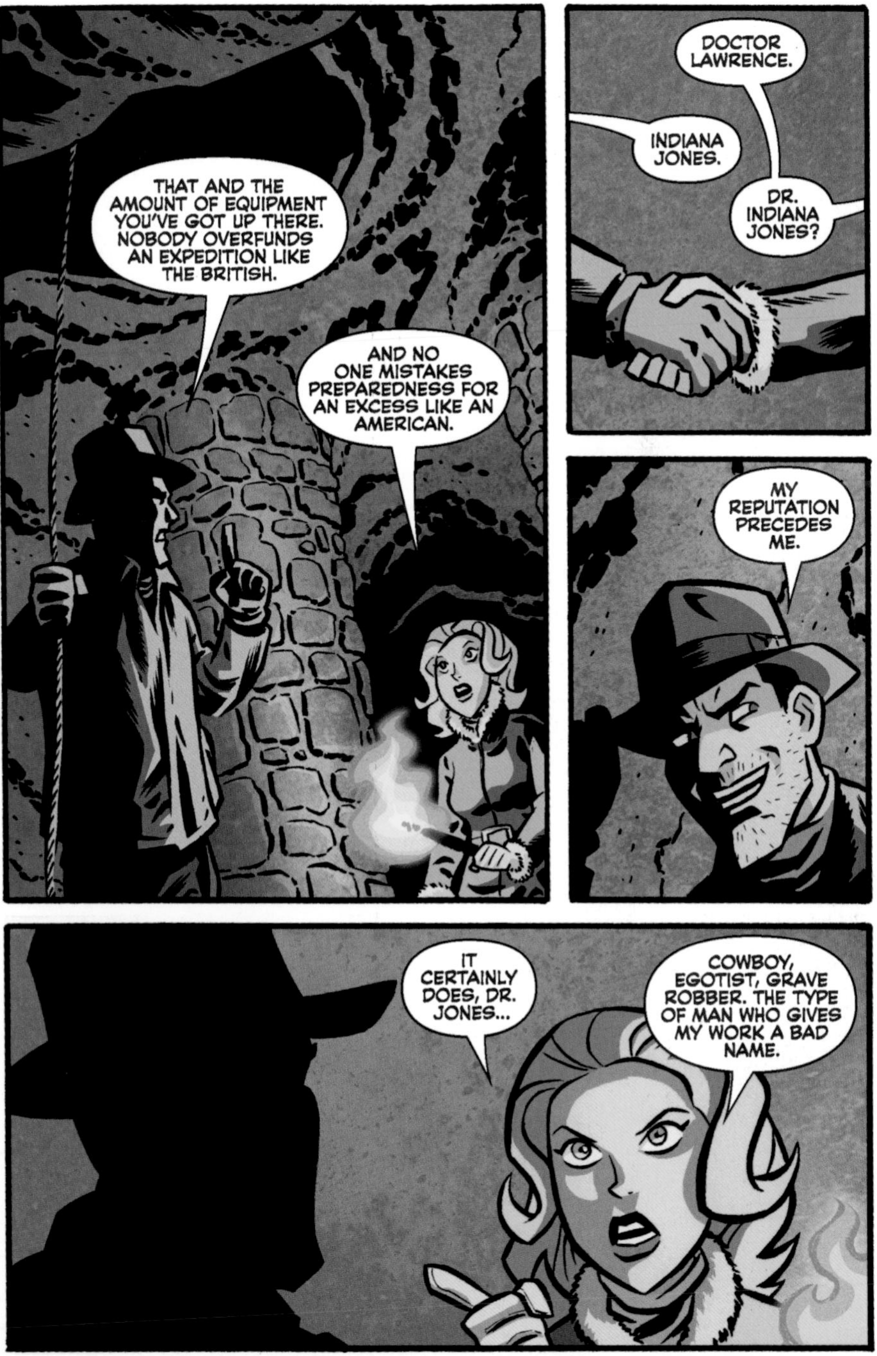
THAT AND THE AMOUNT OF EQUIPMENT YOU'VE GOT UP THERE. NOBODY OVERFUNDS AN EXPEDITION LIKE THE BRITISH.
AND NO ONE MISTAKES PREPAREDNESS FOR AN EXCESS LIKE AN AMERICAN.
DOCTOR LAWRENCE.
INDIANA JONES.
DR. INDIANA JONES?
MY REPUTATION PRECEDES ME.
IT CERTAINLY DOES, DR. JONES...
COWBOY, EGOTIST, GRAVE ROBBER. THE TYPE OF MAN WHO GIVES MY WORK A BAD NAME.

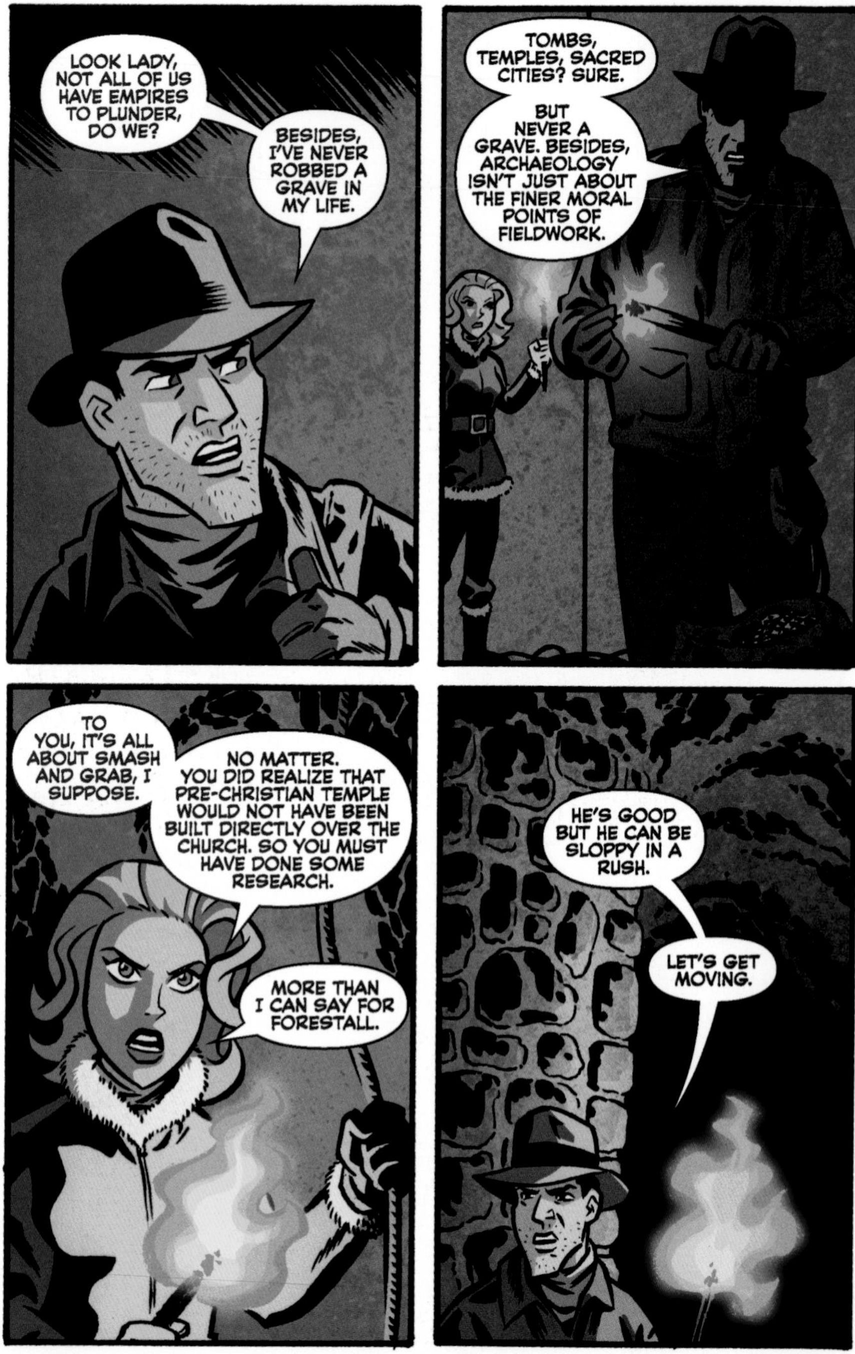
LOOK LADY, NOT ALL OF US HAVE EMPIRES TO PLUNDER, DO WE?
BESIDES, I'VE NEVER ROBBED A GRAVE IN MY LIFE.
TOMBS, TEMPLES, SACRED CITIES? SURE.
BUT NEVER A GRAVE. BESIDES, ARCHAEOLOGY ISN'T JUST ABOUT THE FINER MORAL POINTS OF FIELDWORK.
TO YOU, IT'S ALL ABOUT SMASH AND GRAB, I SUPPOSE.
NO MATTER. YOU DID REALIZE THAT PRE-CHRISTIAN TEMPLE WOULD NOT HAVE BEEN BUILT DIRECTLY OVER THE CHURCH. SO YOU MUST HAVE DONE SOME RESEARCH.
MORE THAN I CAN SAY FOR FORESTALL.
HE'S GOOD BUT HE CAN BE SLOPPY IN A RUSH.
LET'S GET MOVING.

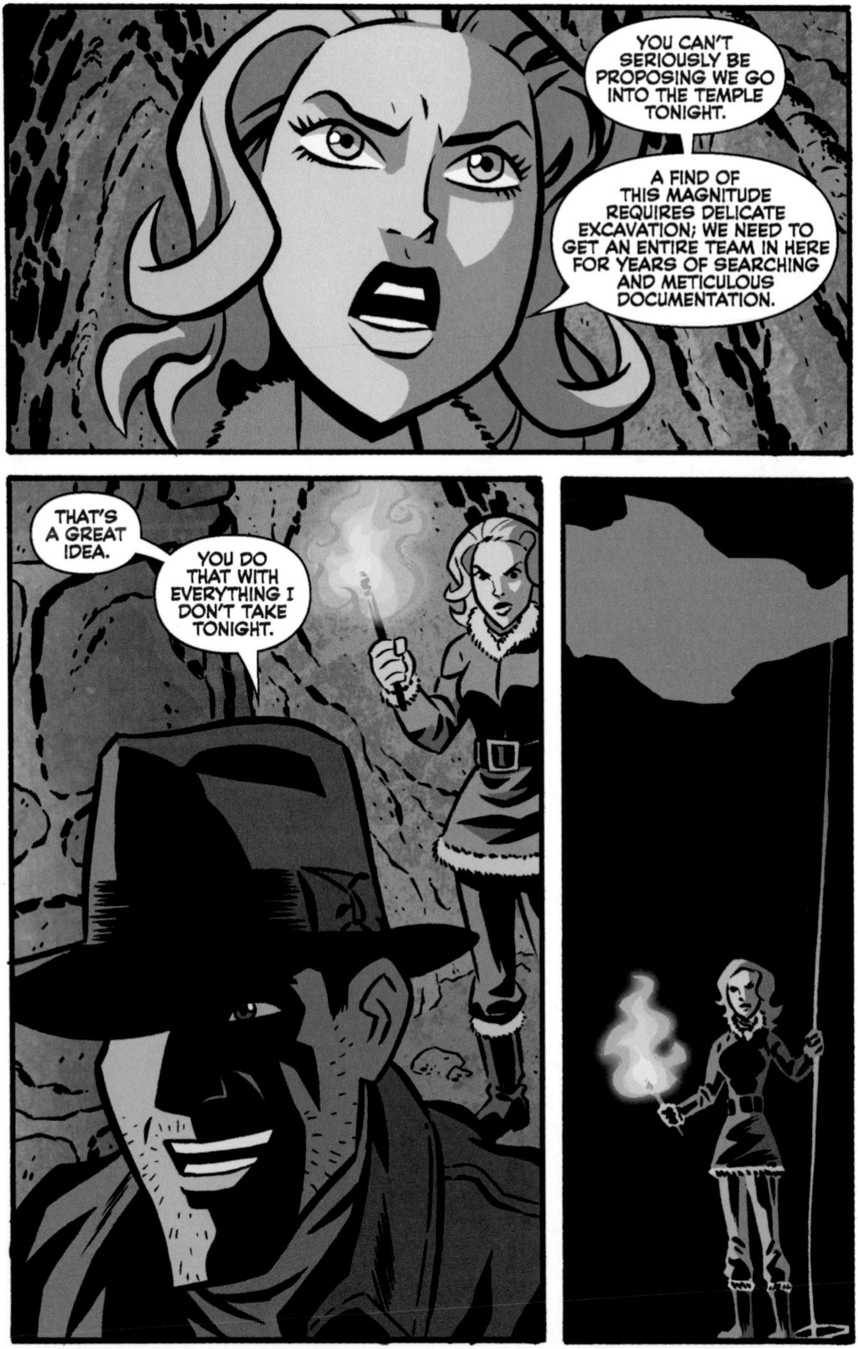
YOU CAN'T SERIOUSLY BE PROPOSING WE GO INTO THE TEMPLE TONIGHT.
A FIND OF THIS MAGNITUDE REQUIRES DELICATE EXCAVATION; WE NEED TO GET AN ENTIRE TEAM IN HERE FOR YEARS OF SEARCHING AND METICULOUS DOCUMENTATION.
THAT'S A GREAT IDEA.
YOU DO THAT WITH EVERYTHING I DON'T TAKE TONIGHT.

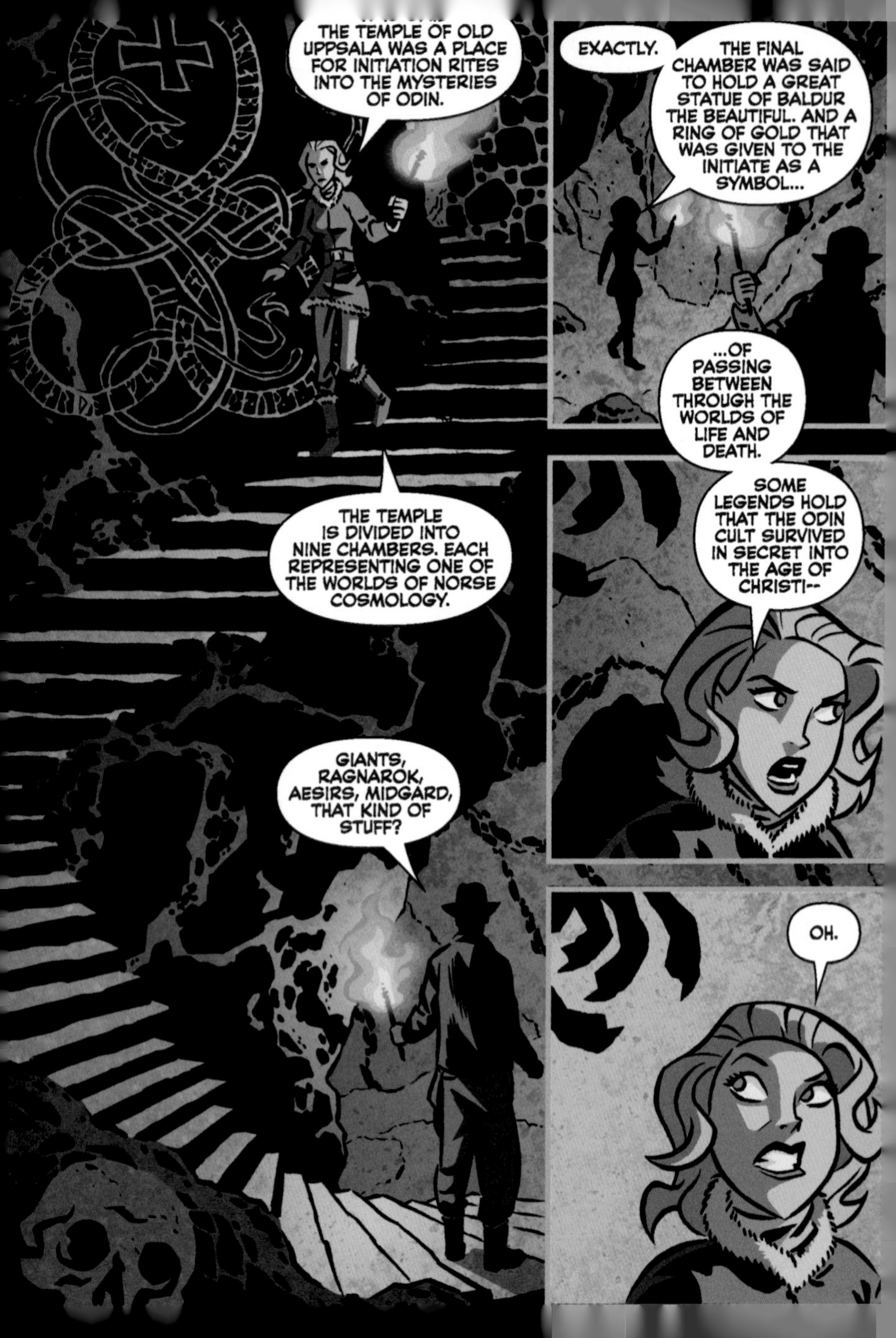
THE TEMPLE OF OLD UPPSALA WAS A PLACE FOR INITIATION RITES INTO THE MYSTERIES OF ODIN.
THE TEMPLE IS DIVIDED INTO NINE CHAMBERS. EACH REPRESENTING ONE OF THE WORLDS OF NORSE COSMOLOGY.
GIANTS, RAGNAROK, AESIRS, MIDGARD, THAT KIND OF STUFF?
EXACTLY.
THE FINAL CHAMBER WAS SAID TO HOLD A GREAT STATUE OF BALDUR THE BEAUTIFUL. AND A RING OF GOLD THAT WAS GIVEN TO THE INITIATE AS A SYMBOL...
...OF PASSING BETWEEN THROUGH THE WORLDS OF LIFE AND DEATH.
SOME LEGENDS HOLD THAT THE ODIN CULT SURVIVED IN SECRET INTO THE AGE OF CHRIST!--
OH.

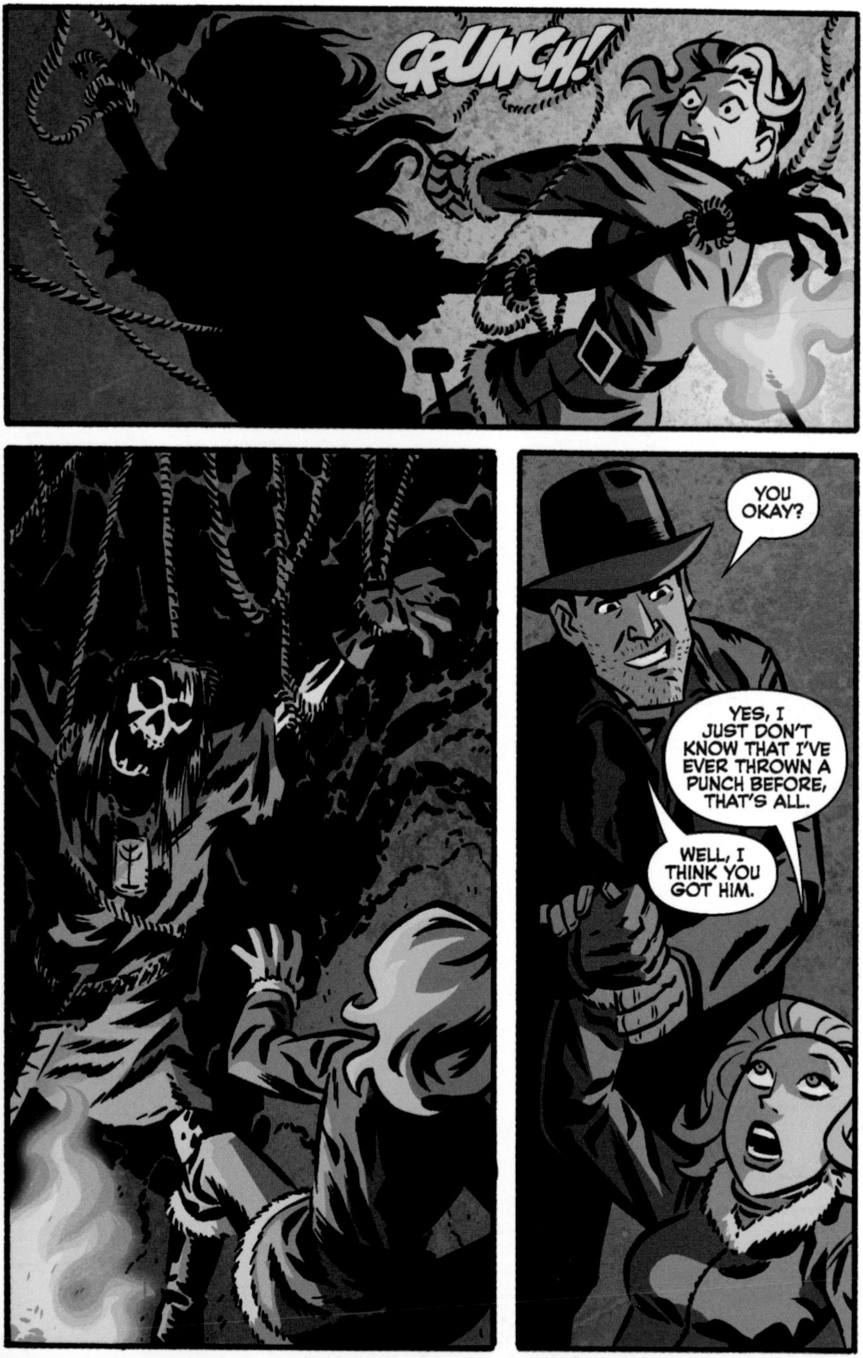
CRUNCH!
YOU OKAY?
YES, I JUST DON'T KNOW THAT I'VE EVER THROWN A PUNCH BEFORE, THAT'S ALL.
WELL, I THINK YOU GOT HIM.

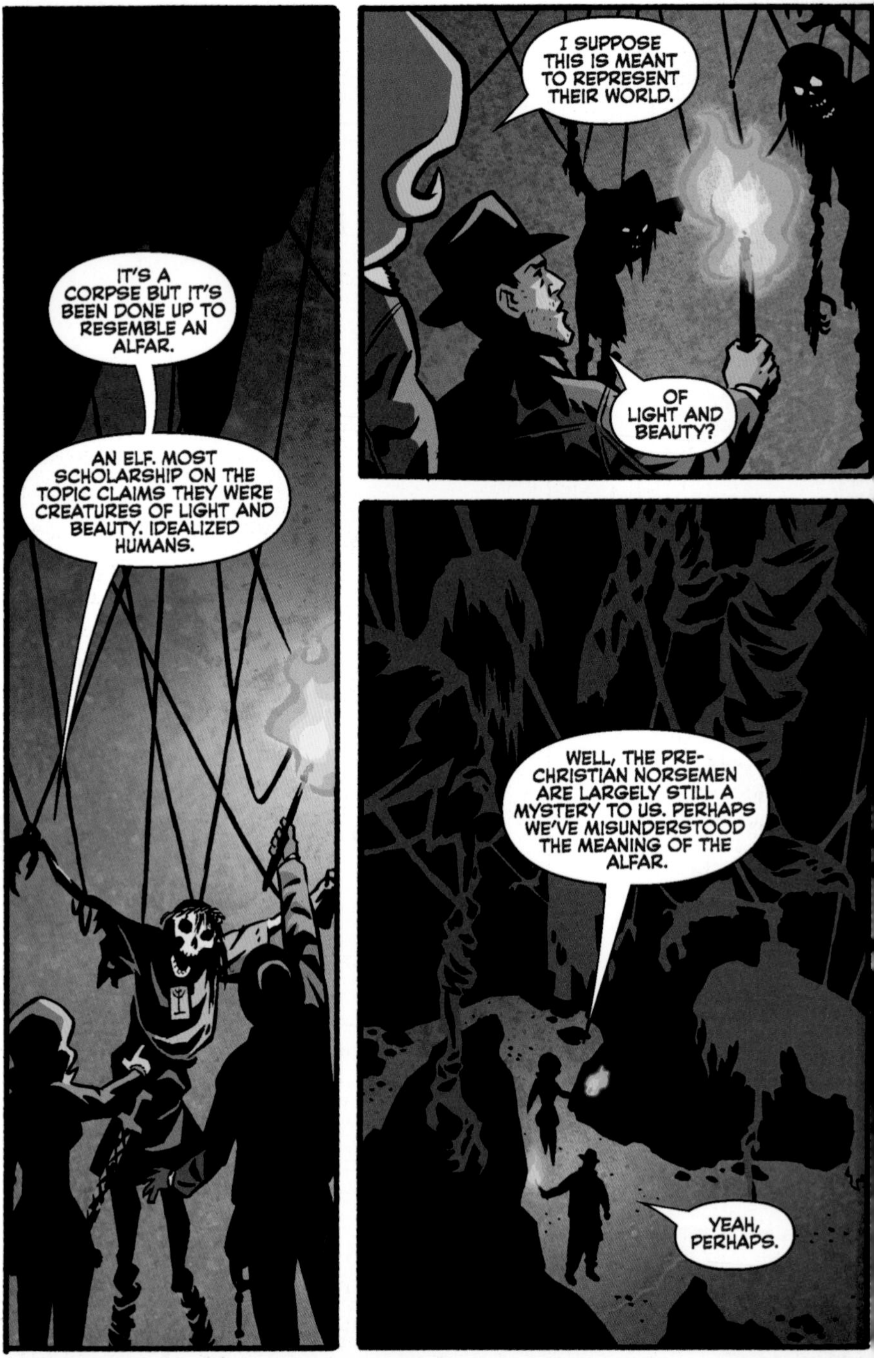
IT'S A CORPSE BUT IT'S BEEN DONE UP TO RESEMBLE AN ALFAR.
AN ELF. MOST SCHOLARSHIP ON THE TOPIC CLAIMS THEY WERE CREATURES OF LIGHT AND BEAUTY. IDEALIZED HUMANS.
I SUPPOSE THIS IS MEANT TO REPRESENT THEIR WORLD.
OF LIGHT AND BEAUTY?
WELL, THE PRE-CHRISTIAN NORSEMEN ARE LARGELY STILL A MYSTERY TO US. PERHAPS WE'VE MISUNDERSTOOD THE MEANING OF THE ALFAR.
YEAH, PERHAPS.

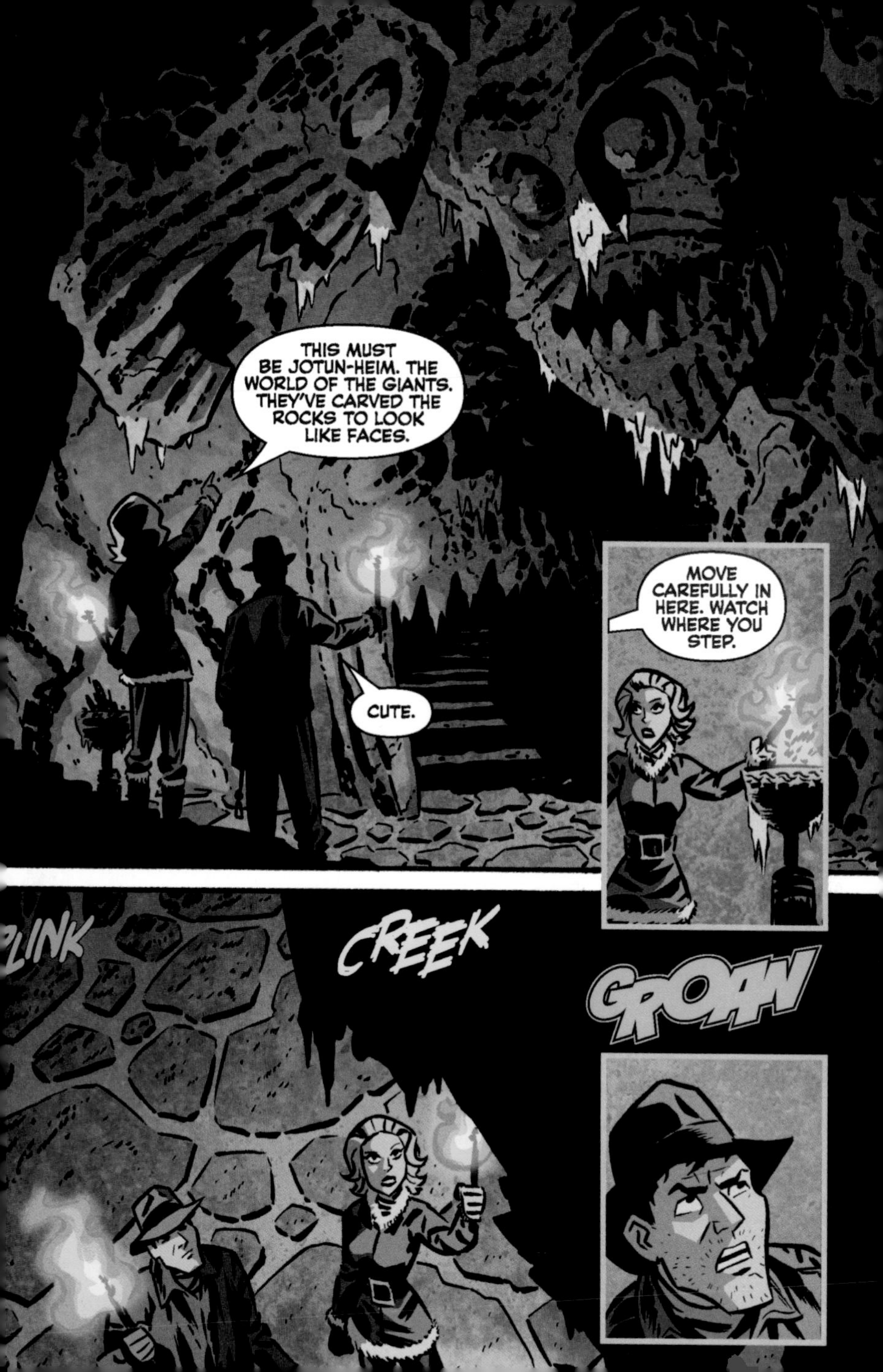
THIS MUST BE JOTUN-HEIM. THE WORLD OF THE GIANTS. THEY'VE CARVED THE ROCKS TO LOOK LIKE FACES.
CUTE.
MOVE CAREFULLY IN HERE. WATCH WHERE YOU STEP.
LINK
CREEK
GROAN

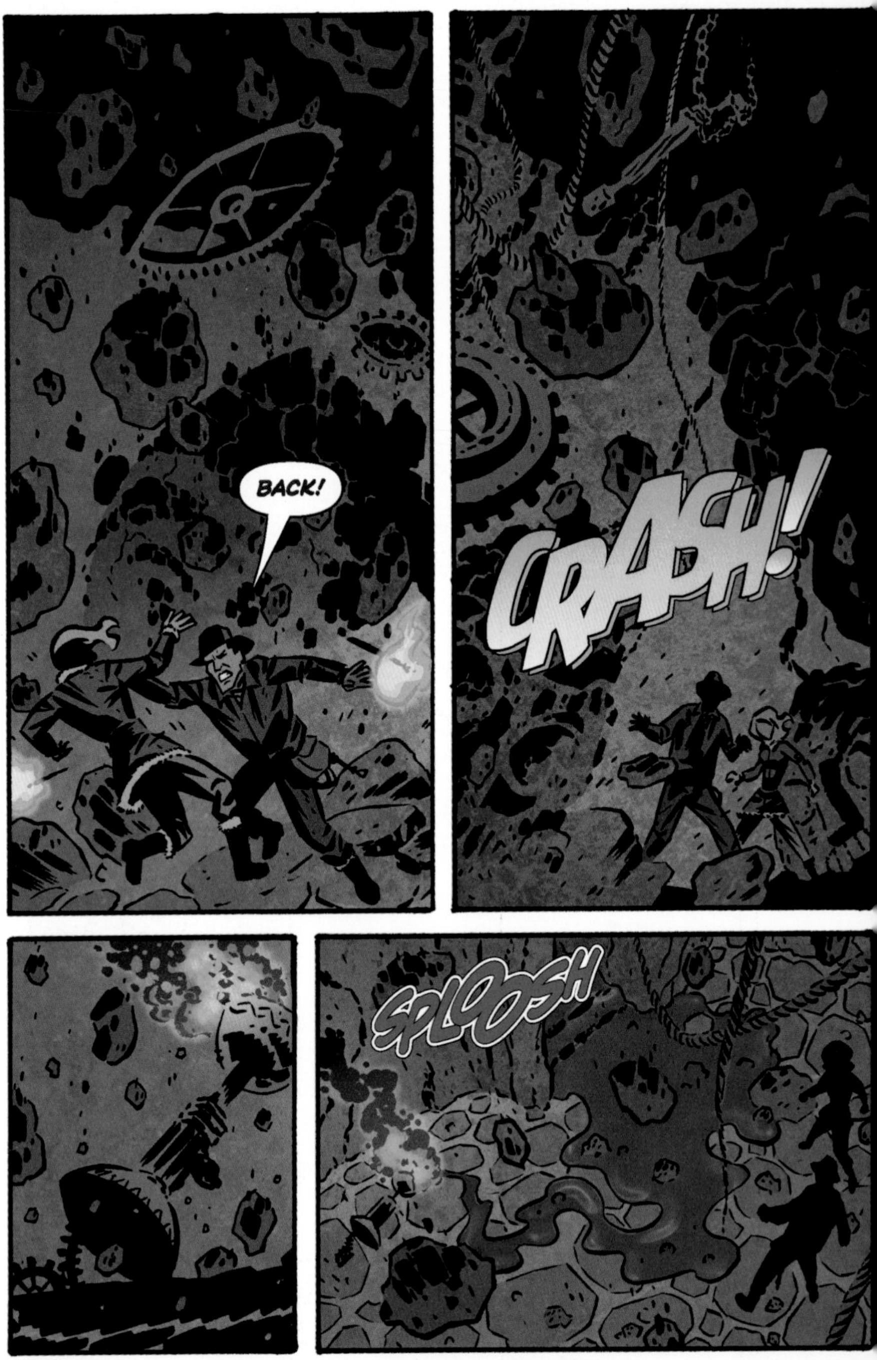
BACK!
CRASH!
SPLOOSH

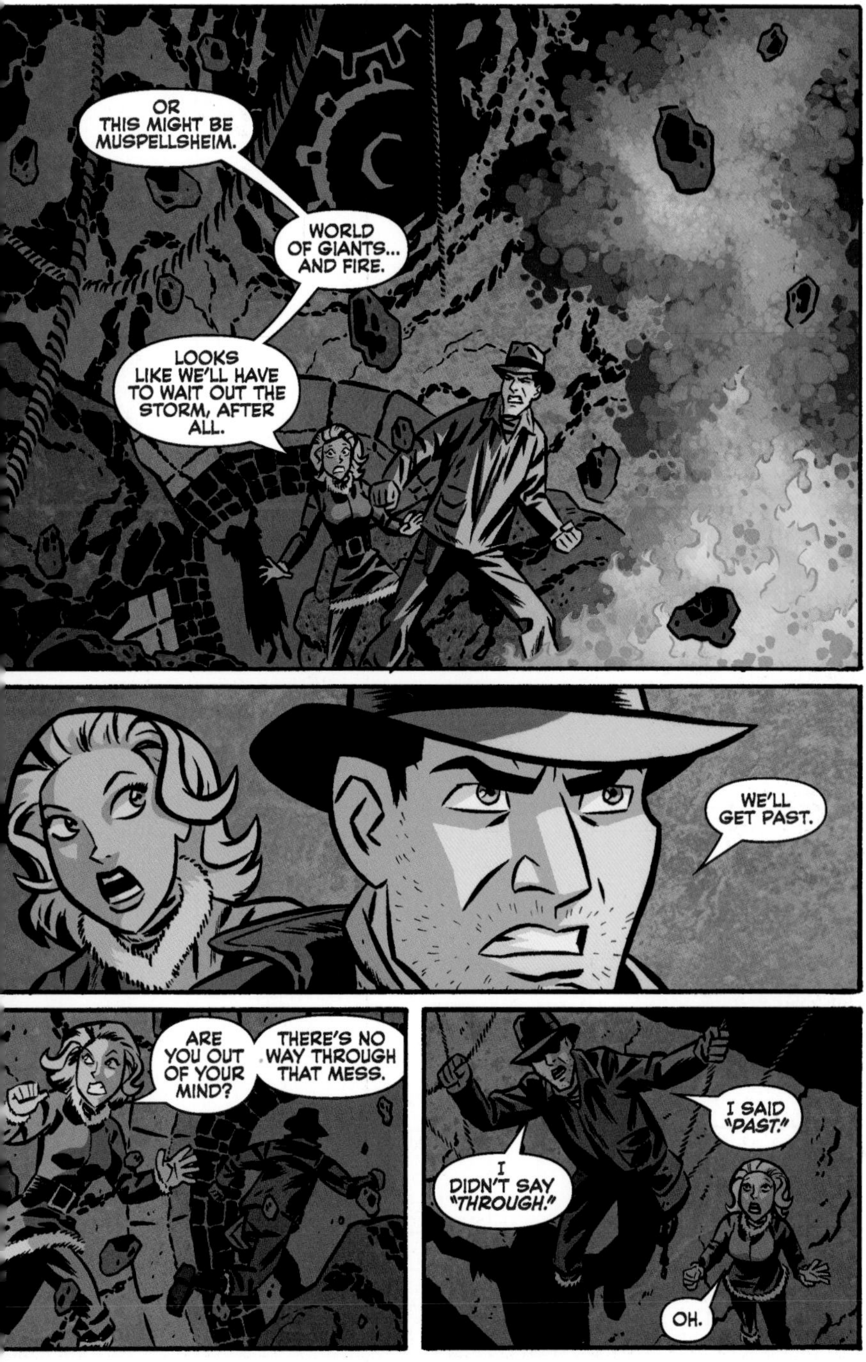
OR THIS MIGHT BE MUSPELLSHEIM.
WORLD OF GIANTS... AND FIRE.
LOOKS LIKE WE'LL HAVE TO WAIT OUT THE STORM, AFTER ALL.
WE'LL GET PAST.
ARE YOU OUT OF YOUR MIND?
THERE'S NO WAY THROUGH THAT MESS.
I SAID "PAST."
I DIDN'T SAY "THROUGH."
OH.

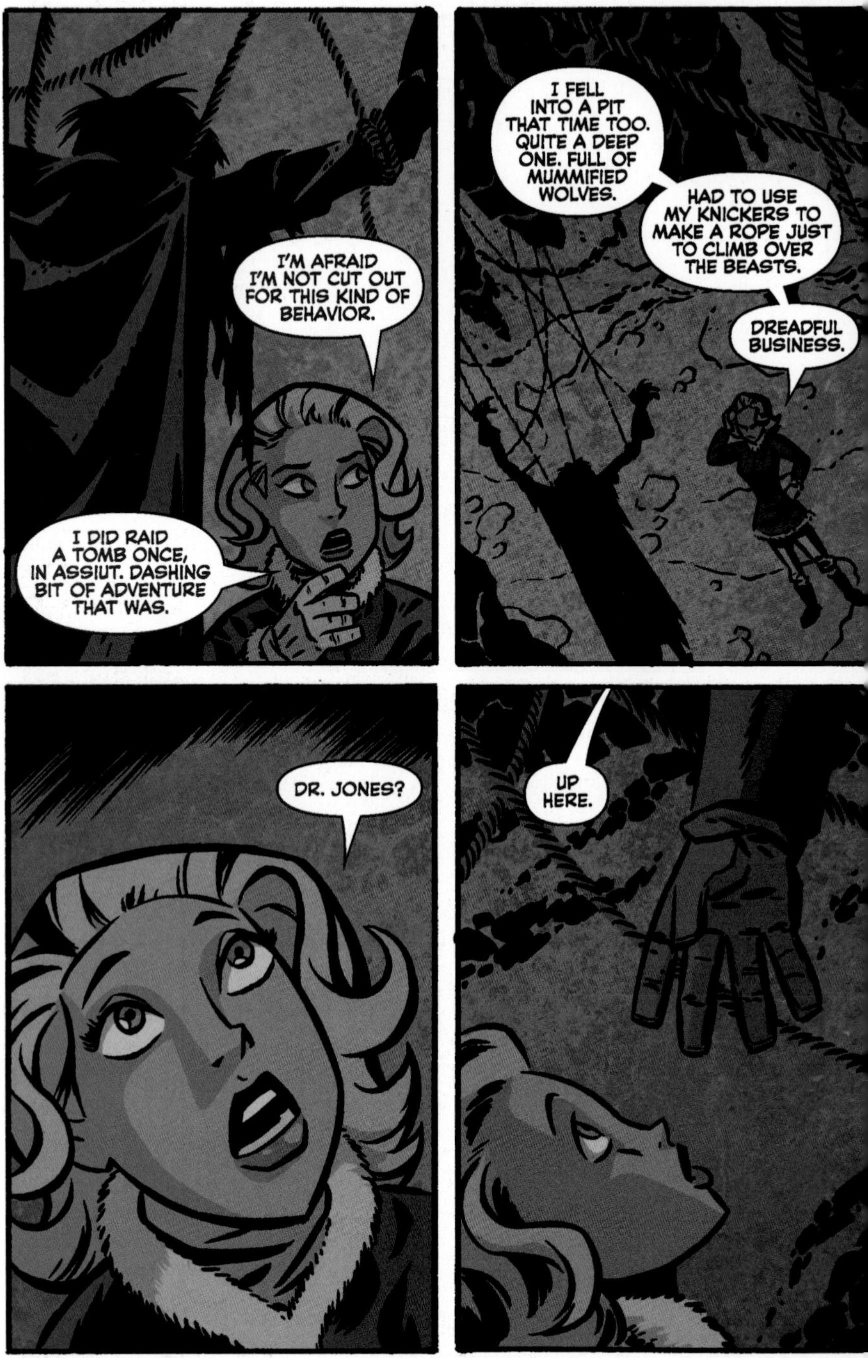
I'M AFRAID I'M NOT CUT OUT FOR THIS KIND OF BEHAVIOR.
I DID RAID A TOMB ONCE, IN ASSIUT. DASHING BIT OF ADVENTURE THAT WAS.
I FELL INTO A PIT THAT TIME TOO. QUITE A DEEP ONE. FULL OF MUMMIFIED WOLVES.
HAD TO USE MY KNICKERS TO MAKE A ROPE JUST TO CLIMB OVER THE BEASTS.
DREADFUL BUSINESS.
DR. JONES?
UP HERE.

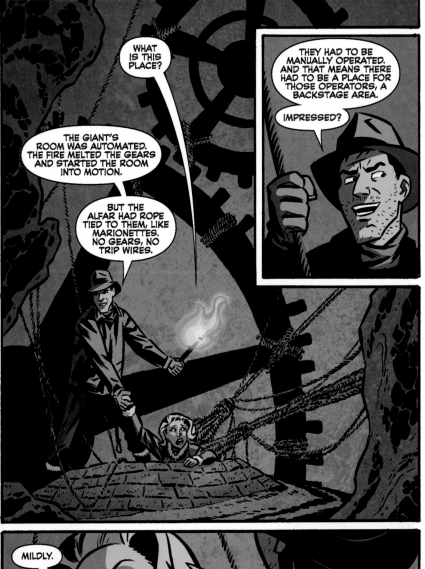

WHAT IS THIS PLACE?

THEY HAD TO BE MANUALLY OPERATED. AND THAT MEANS THERE HAD TO BE A PLACE FOR THOSE OPERATORS, A BACKSTAGE AREA.

IMPRESSED?

THE GIANT'S ROOM WAS AUTOMATED. THE FIRE MELTED THE GEARS AND STARTED THE ROOM INTO MOTION.

BUT THE ALFAR HAD ROPE TIED TO THEM, LIKE MARIONETTES. NO GEARS, NO TRIP WIRES.

MILDLY.

BUT MORE WITH THE ANCIENT NORSEMEN. LOOK AT THIS PLACE...

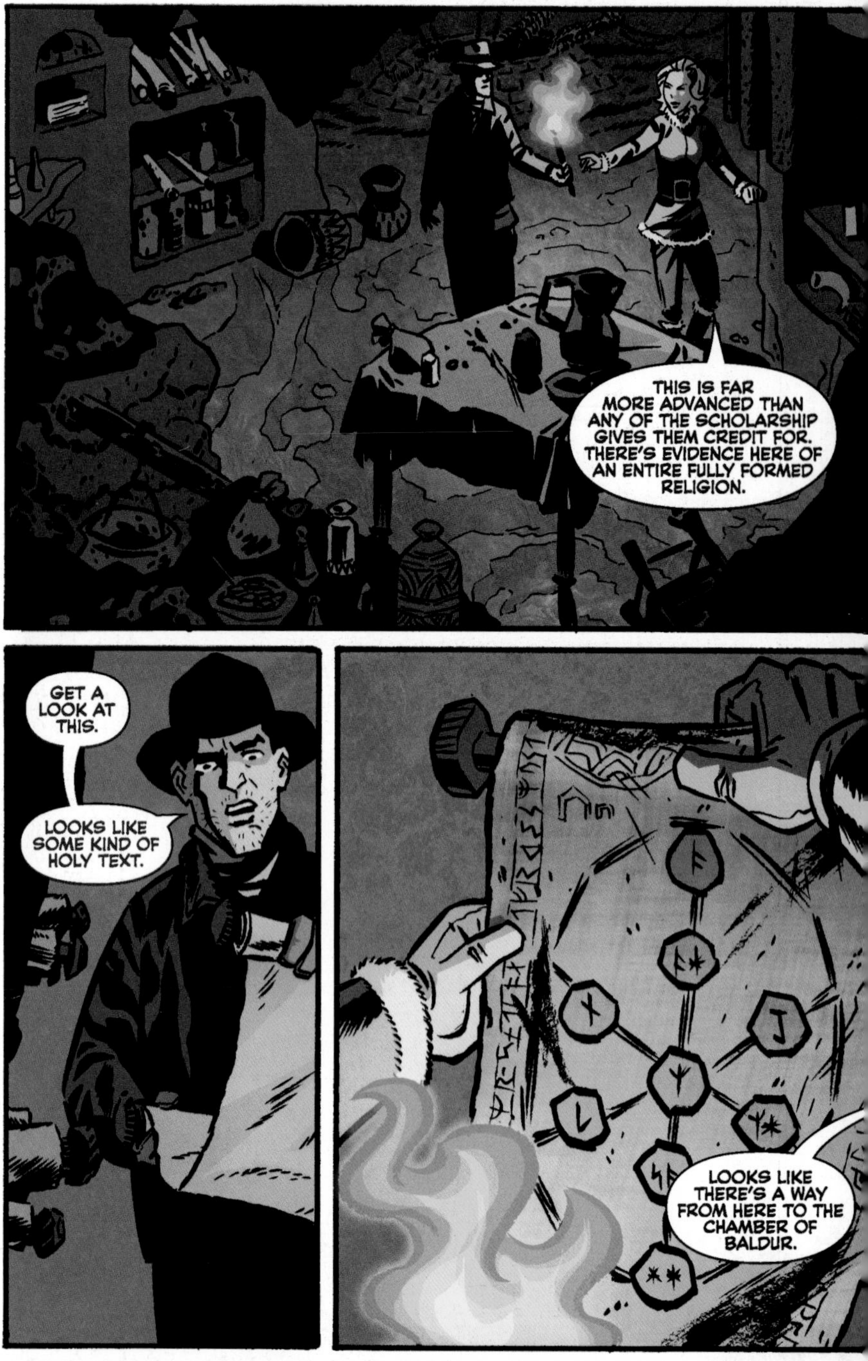
THIS IS FAR MORE ADVANCED THAN ANY OF THE SCHOLARSHIP GIVES THEM CREDIT FOR. THERE'S EVIDENCE HERE OF AN ENTIRE FULLY FORMED RELIGION.
GET A LOOK AT THIS.
LOOKS LIKE SOME KIND OF HOLY TEXT.
LOOKS LIKE THERE'S A WAY FROM HERE TO THE CHAMBER OF BALDUR.

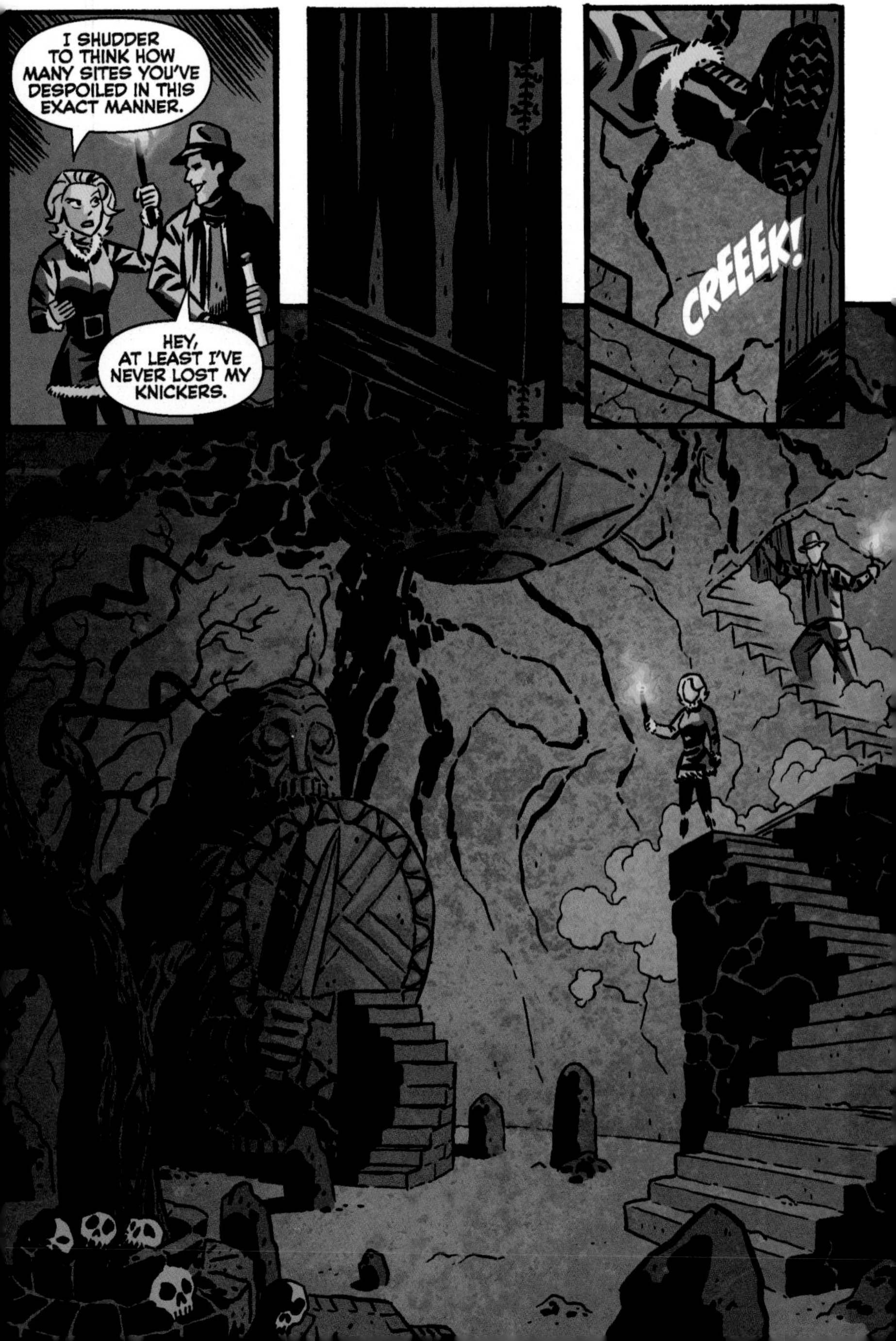
I SHUDDER TO THINK HOW MANY SITES YOU'VE DESPOILED IN THIS EXACT MANNER.
HEY, AT LEAST I'VE NEVER LOST MY KNICKERS.
CREEEK!

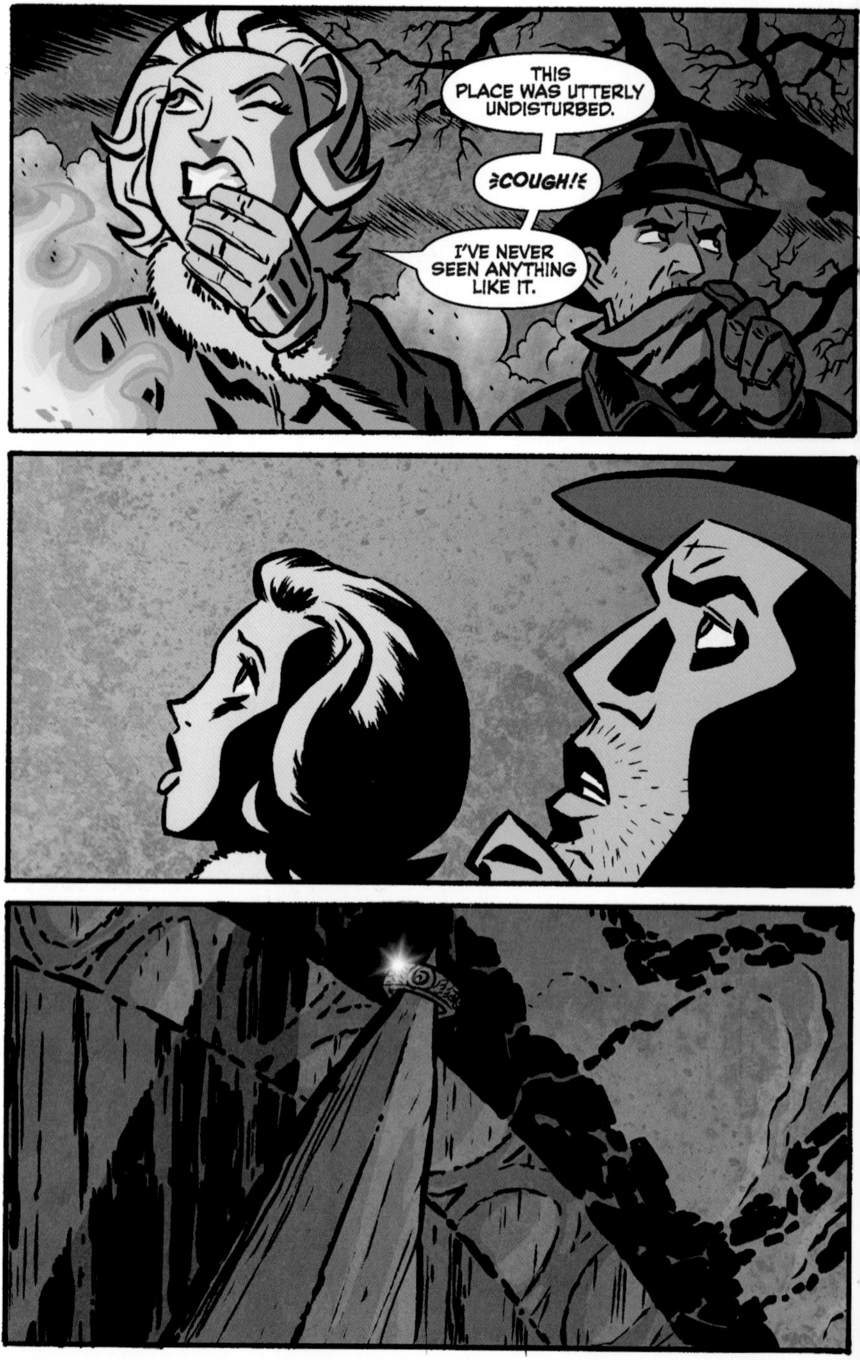
THIS PLACE WAS UTTERLY UNDISTURBED.
COUGH!
I'VE NEVER SEEN ANYTHING LIKE IT.

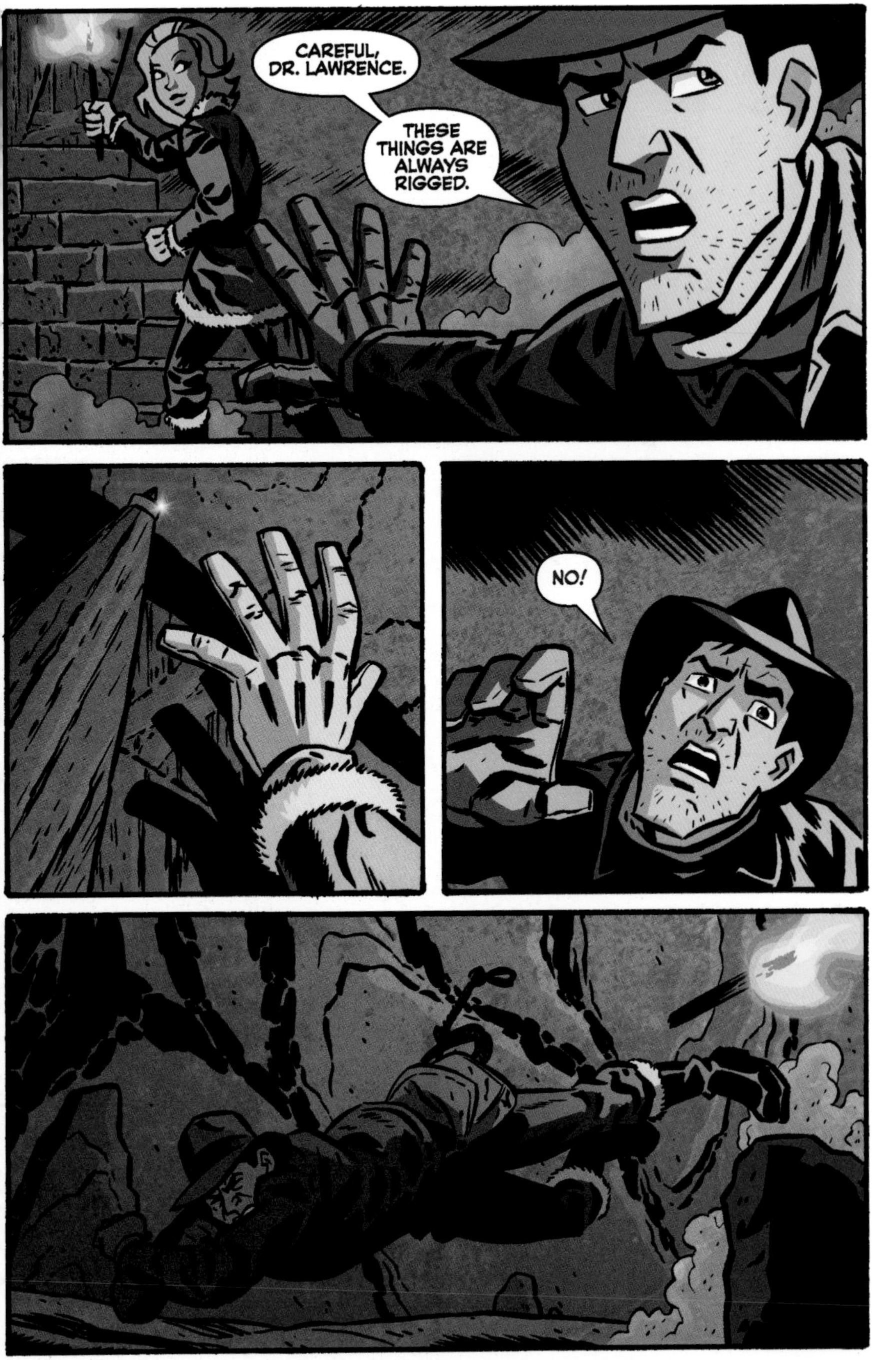
CAREFUL, DR. LAWRENCE.
THESE THINGS ARE ALWAYS RIGGED.
NO!

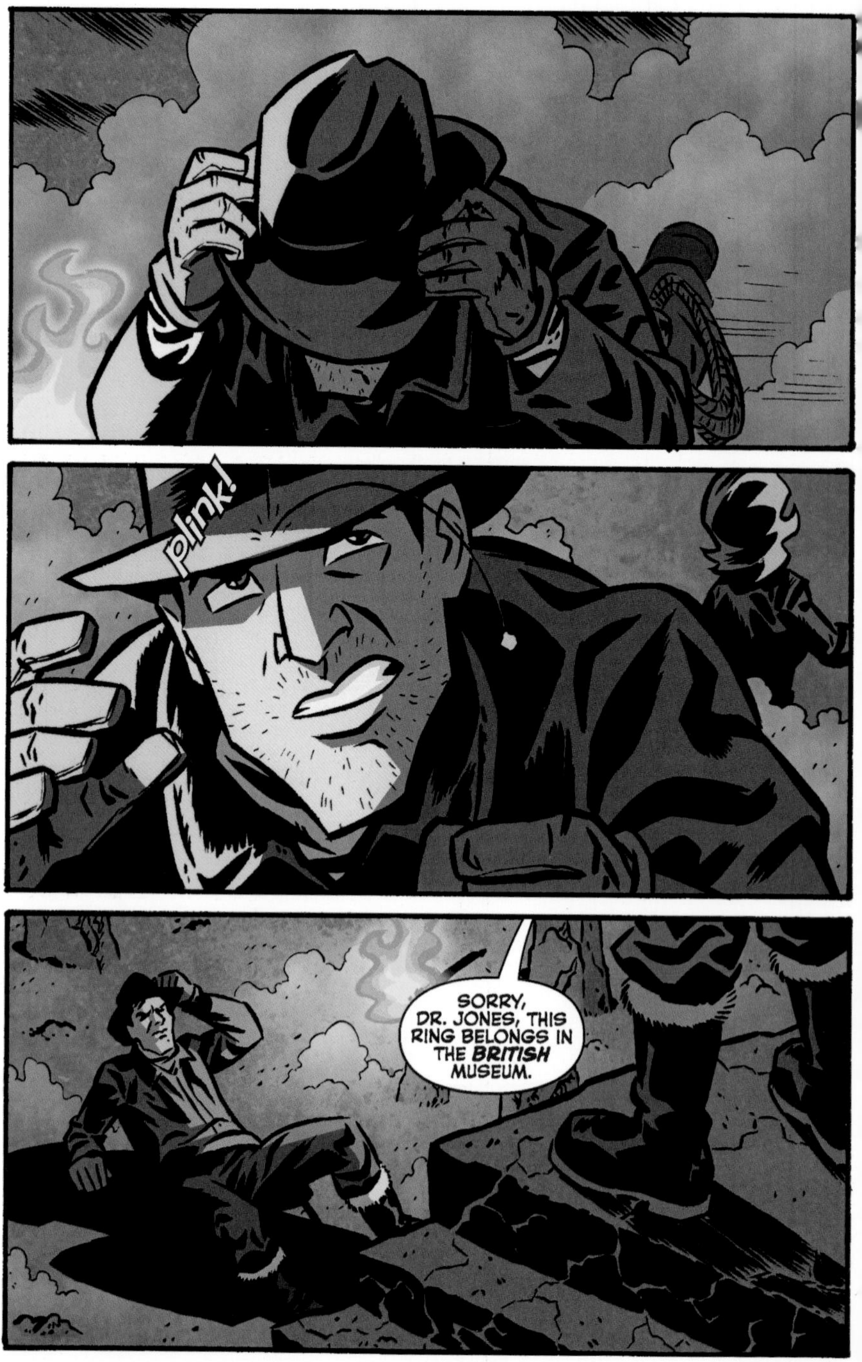
plink!
SORRY, DR. JONES, THIS RING BELONGS IN THE BRITISH MUSEUM.

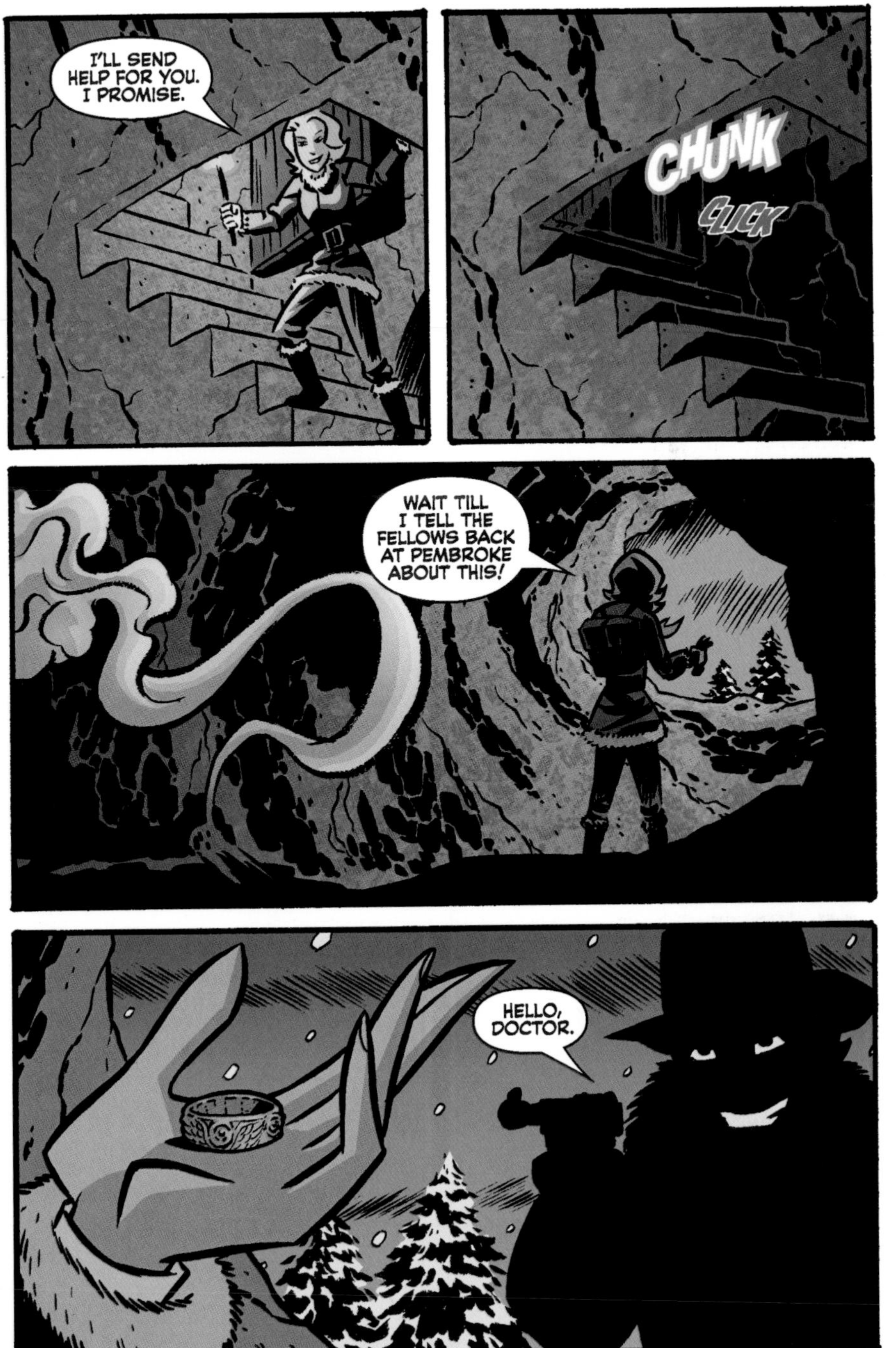
I'LL SEND HELP FOR YOU. I PROMISE.
CHUNK
CLICK
WAIT TILL I TELL THE FELLOWS BACK AT PEMBROKE ABOUT THIS!
HELLO, DOCTOR.

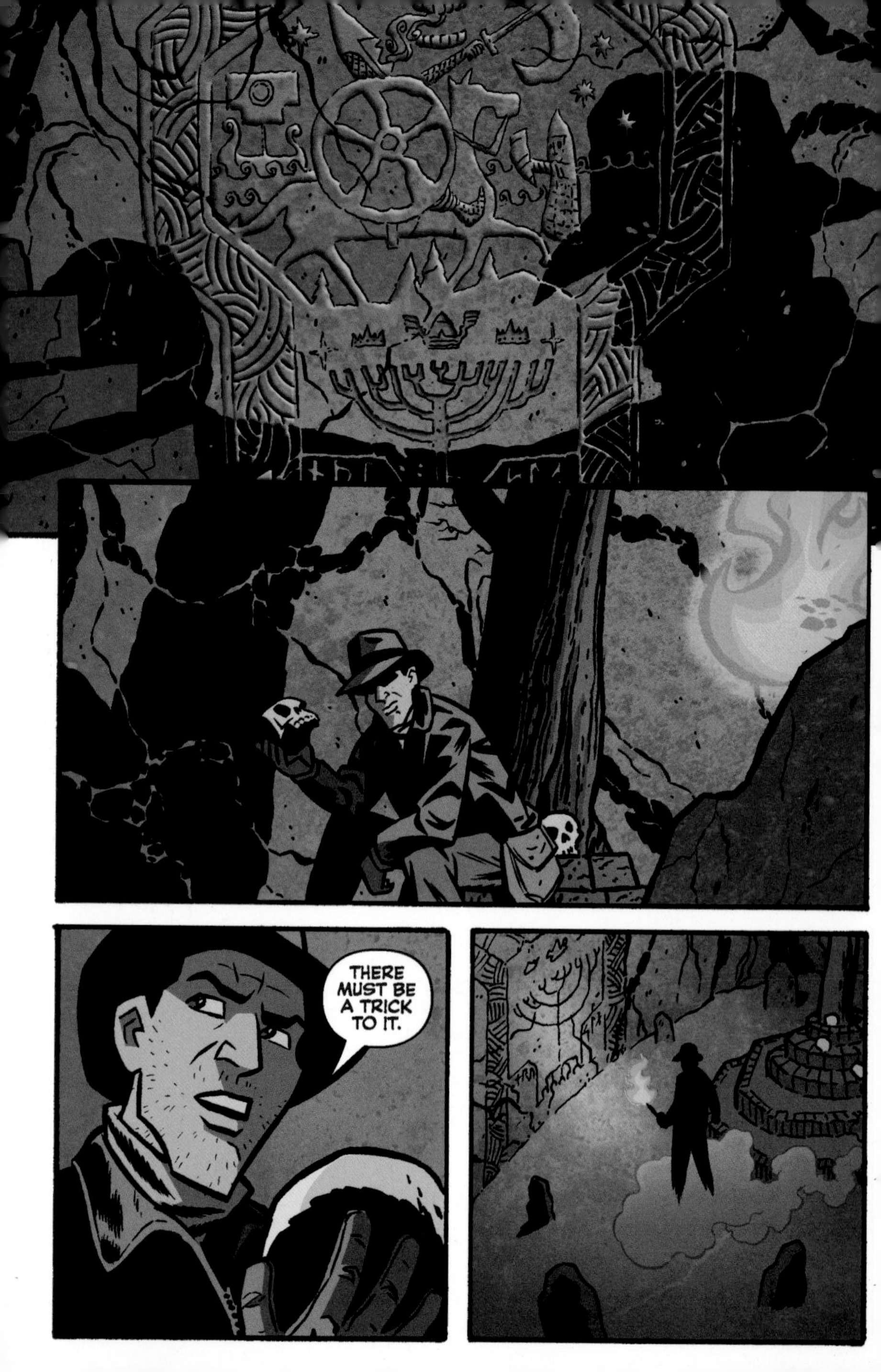
THERE MUST BE A TRICK TO IT.

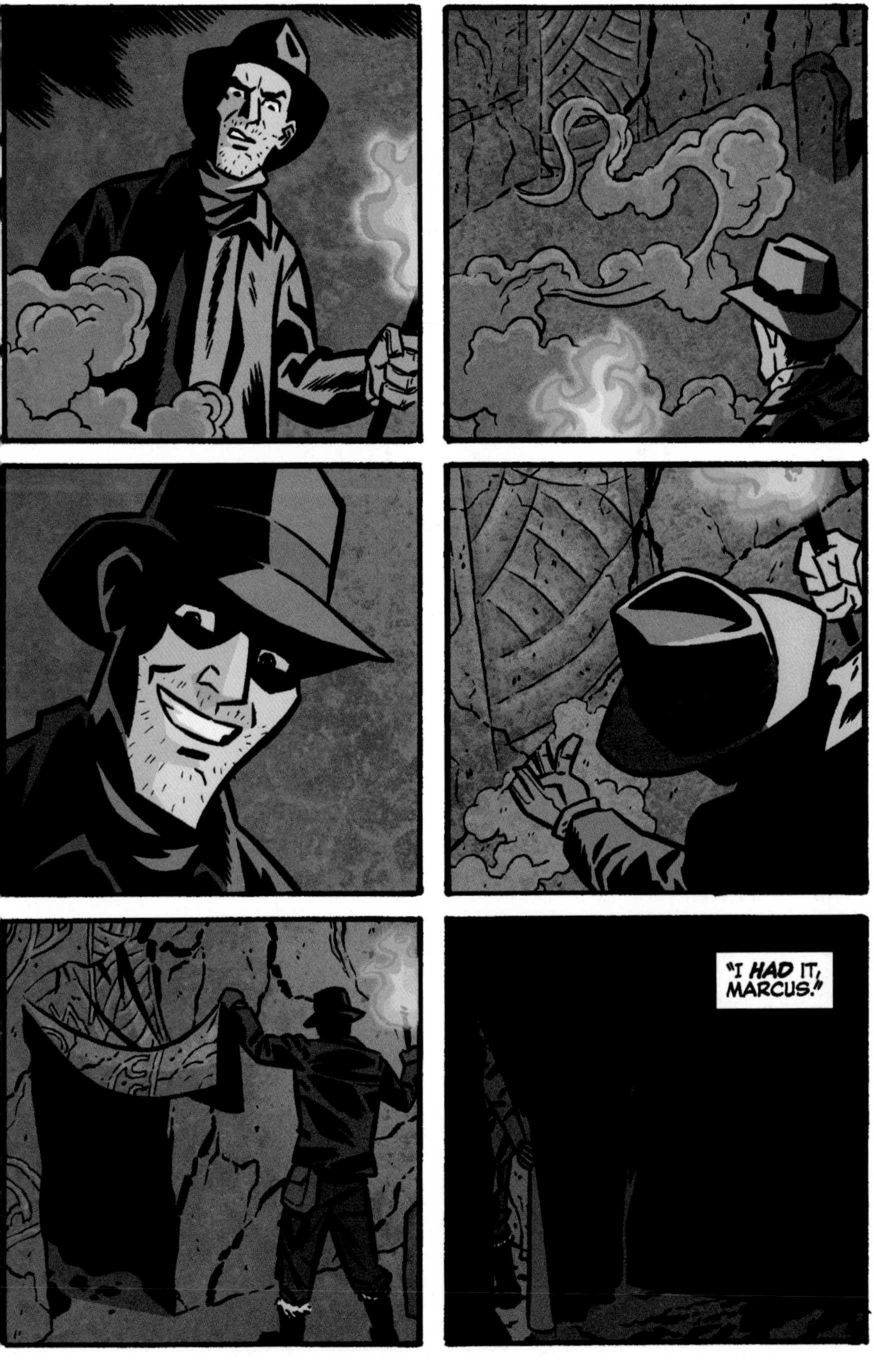
"I HAD IT, MARCUS."

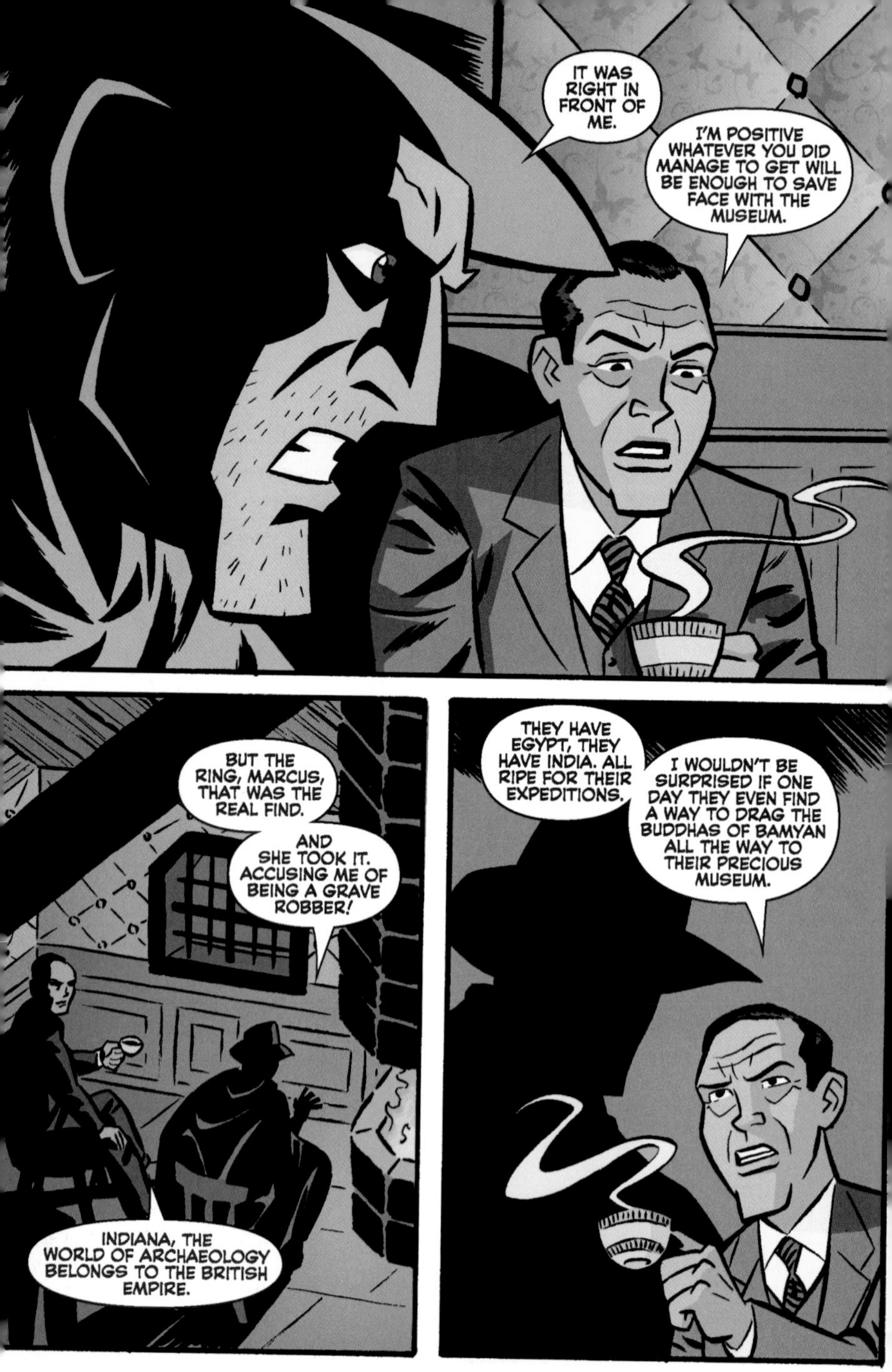
IT WAS RIGHT IN FRONT OF ME.
I'M POSITIVE WHATEVER YOU DID MANAGE TO GET WILL BE ENOUGH TO SAVE FACE WITH THE MUSEUM.
BUT THE RING, MARCUS, THAT WAS THE REAL FIND.
AND SHE TOOK IT. ACCUSING ME OF BEING A GRAVE ROBBER!
INDIANA, THE WORLD OF ARCHAEOLOGY BELONGS TO THE BRITISH EMPIRE.
THEY HAVE EGYPT, THEY HAVE INDIA. ALL RIPE FOR THEIR EXPEDITIONS.
I WOULDN'T BE SURPRISED IF ONE DAY THEY EVEN FIND A WAY TO DRAG THE BUDDHAS OF BAMYAN ALL THE WAY TO THEIR PRECIOUS MUSEUM.

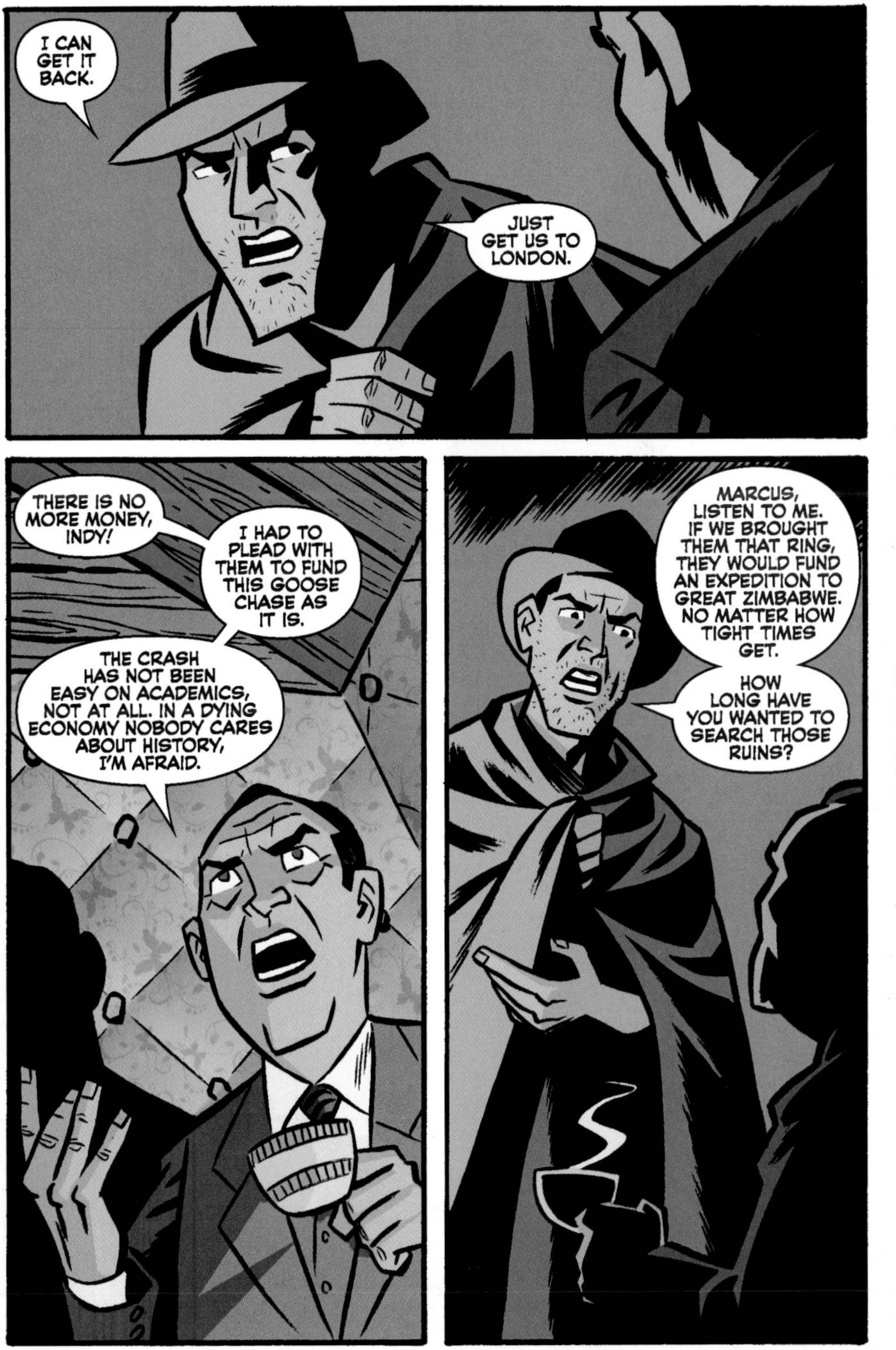
I CAN GET IT BACK.
JUST GET US TO LONDON.
THERE IS NO MORE MONEY, INDY!
I HAD TO PLEAD WITH THEM TO FUND THIS GOOSE CHASE AS IT IS.
THE CRASH HAS NOT BEEN EASY ON ACADEMICS, NOT AT ALL. IN A DYING ECONOMY NOBODY CARES ABOUT HISTORY, I'M AFRAID.
MARCUS, LISTEN TO ME. IF WE BROUGHT THEM THAT RING, THEY WOULD FUND AN EXPEDITION TO GREAT ZIMBABWE. NO MATTER HOW TIGHT TIMES GET.
HOW LONG HAVE YOU WANTED TO SEARCH THOSE RUINS?

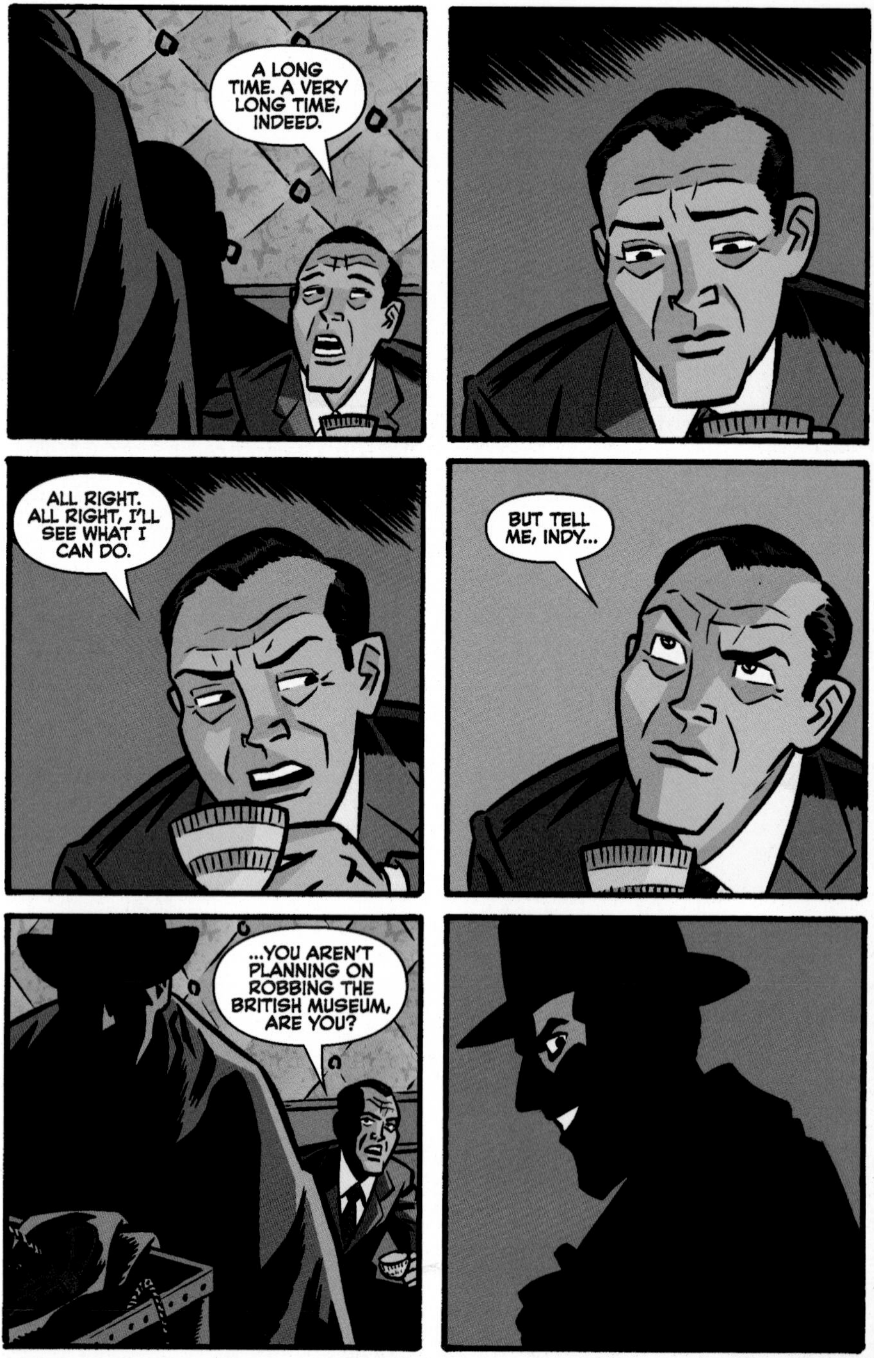
A LONG TIME. A VERY LONG TIME, INDEED.
ALL RIGHT. ALL RIGHT, I'LL SEE WHAT I CAN DO.
BUT TELL ME, INDY...
...YOU AREN'T PLANNING ON ROBBING THE BRITISH MUSEUM, ARE YOU?

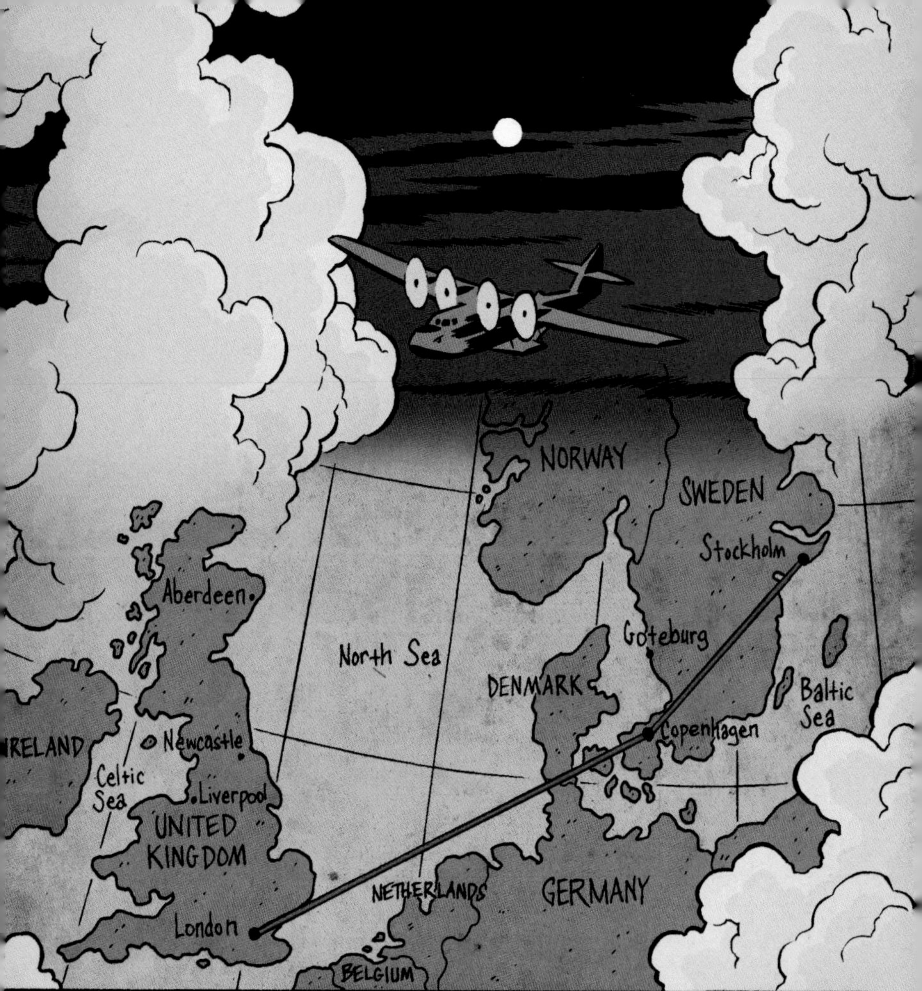
NORWAY
SWEDEN
Stockholm
Aberdeen
North Sea
Goteburg
DENMARK
Baltic Sea
Copenhagen
IRELAND
Newcastle
Celtic Sea
Liverpool
UNITED KINGDOM
NETHERLANDS
GERMANY
London
BELGIUM
FRANCE

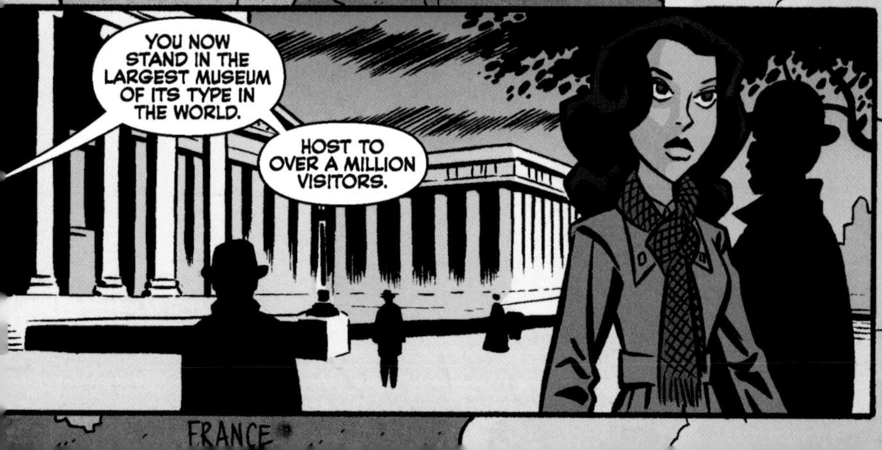
YOU NOW STAND IN THE LARGEST MUSEUM OF ITS TYPE IN THE WORLD.
HOST TO OVER A MILLION VISITORS.

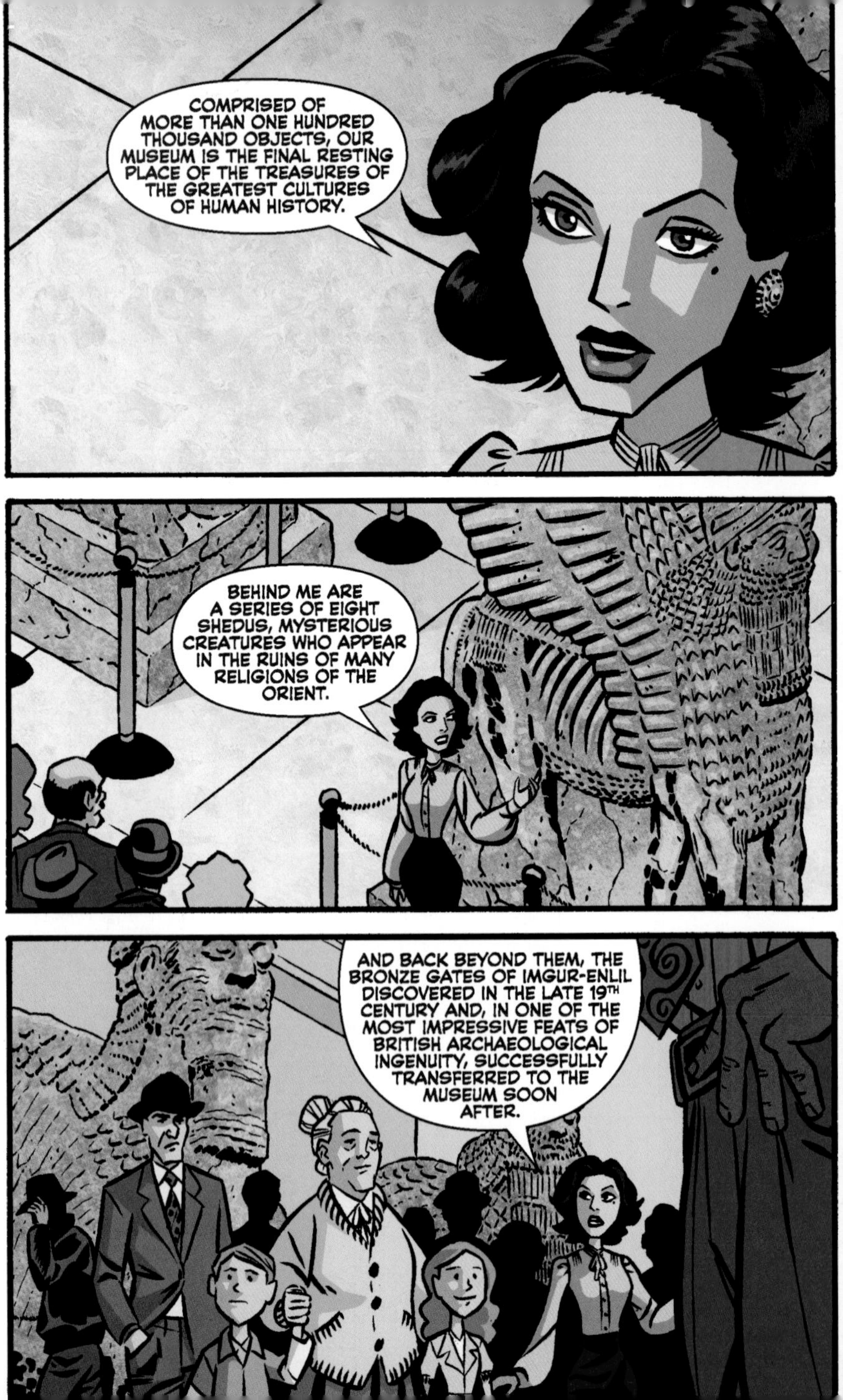
COMPRISED OF MORE THAN ONE HUNDRED THOUSAND OBJECTS, OUR MUSEUM IS THE FINAL RESTING PLACE OF THE TREASURES OF THE GREATEST CULTURES OF HUMAN HISTORY.
BEHIND ME ARE A SERIES OF EIGHT SHEDUS, MYSTERIOUS CREATURES WHO APPEAR IN THE RUINS OF MANY RELIGIONS OF THE ORIENT.
AND BACK BEYOND THEM, THE BRONZE GATES OF IMGUR-ENLIL DISCOVERED IN THE LATE 19TH CENTURY AND, IN ONE OF THE MOST IMPRESSIVE FEATS OF BRITISH ARCHAEOLOGICAL INGENUITY, SUCCESSFULLY TRANSFERRED TO THE MUSEUM SOON AFTER.

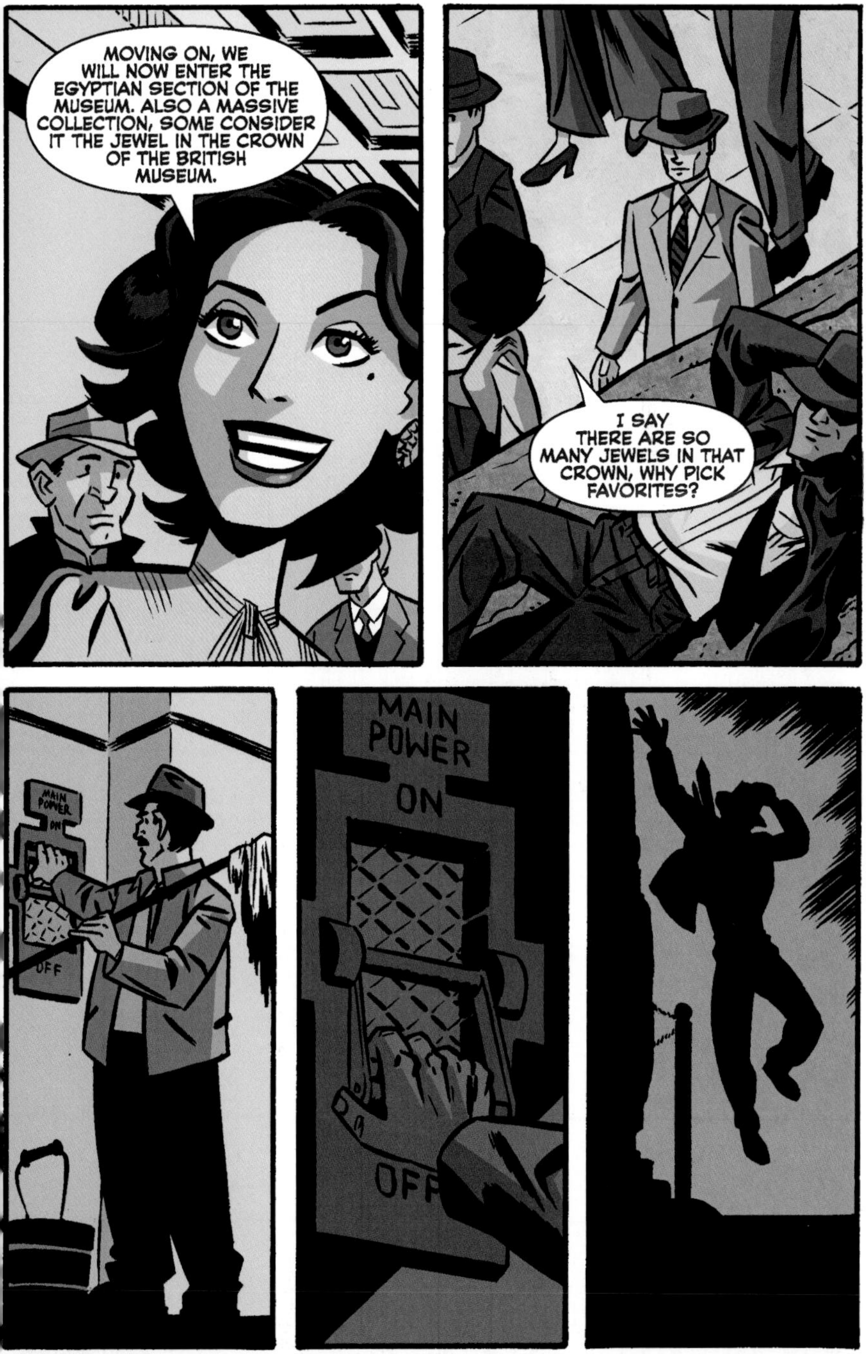
MOVING ON, WE WILL NOW ENTER THE EGYPTIAN SECTION OF THE MUSEUM. ALSO A MASSIVE COLLECTION, SOME CONSIDER IT THE JEWEL IN THE CROWN OF THE BRITISH MUSEUM.
I SAY THERE ARE SO MANY JEWELS IN THAT CROWN, WHY PICK FAVORITES?
MAIN POWER ON
OFF
MAIN POWER
ON
OFF

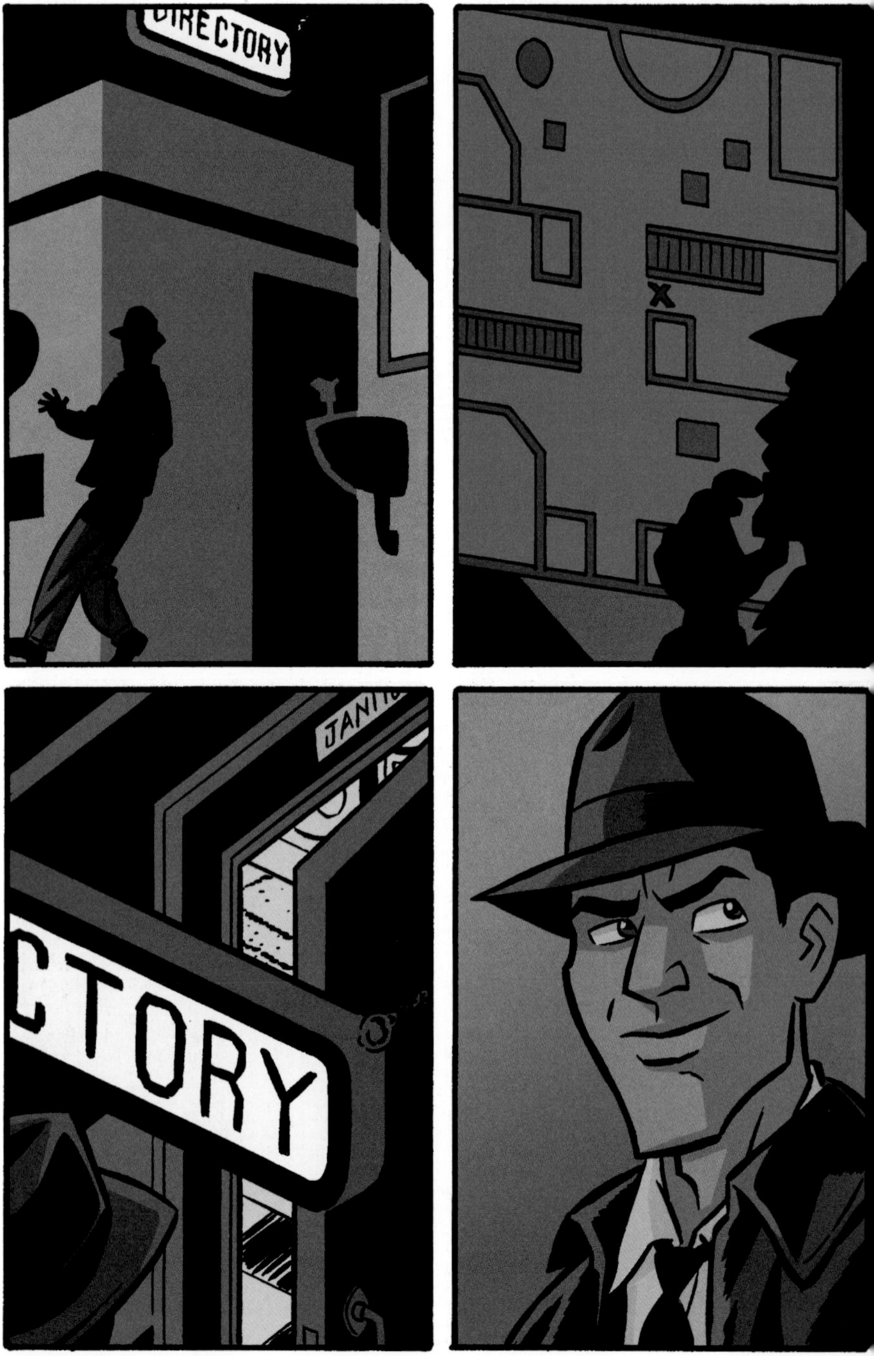
DIRECTORY
JANI
CTORY

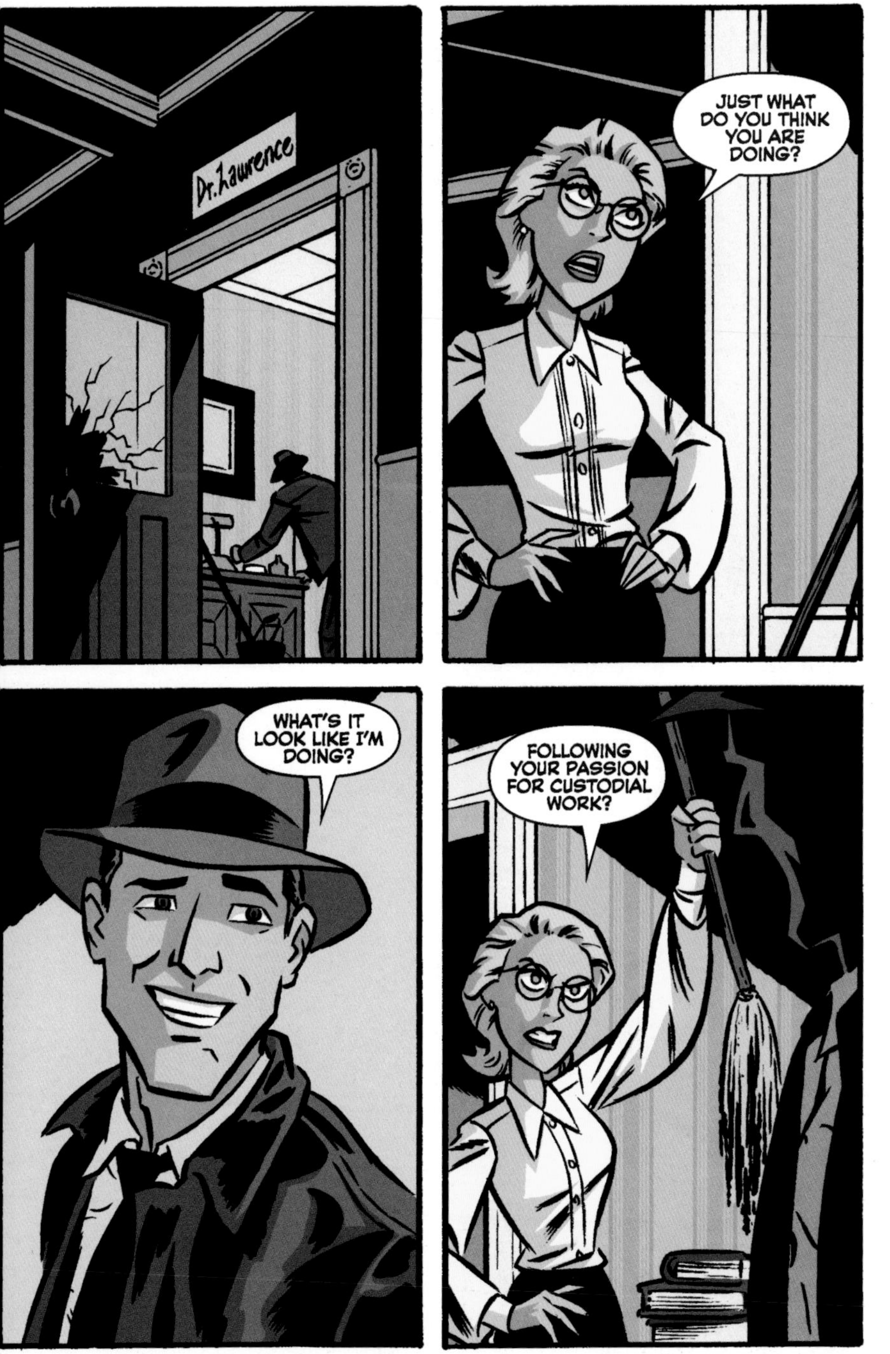
Dr. Lawrence
JUST WHAT DO YOU THINK YOU ARE DOING?
WHAT'S IT LOOK LIKE I'M DOING?
FOLLOWING YOUR PASSION FOR CUSTODIAL WORK?

I'M ROBBING YOU BACK!

WHY?

YOU STOLE THIS FROM *ME*, REMEMBER?

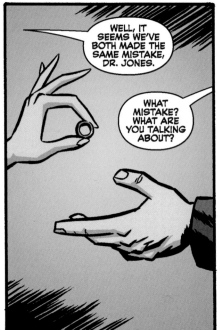

WELL, IT SEEMS WE'VE BOTH MADE THE SAME MISTAKE, DR. JONES.

WHAT MISTAKE? WHAT ARE YOU TALKING ABOUT?

THE SCROLL, DR. JONES.

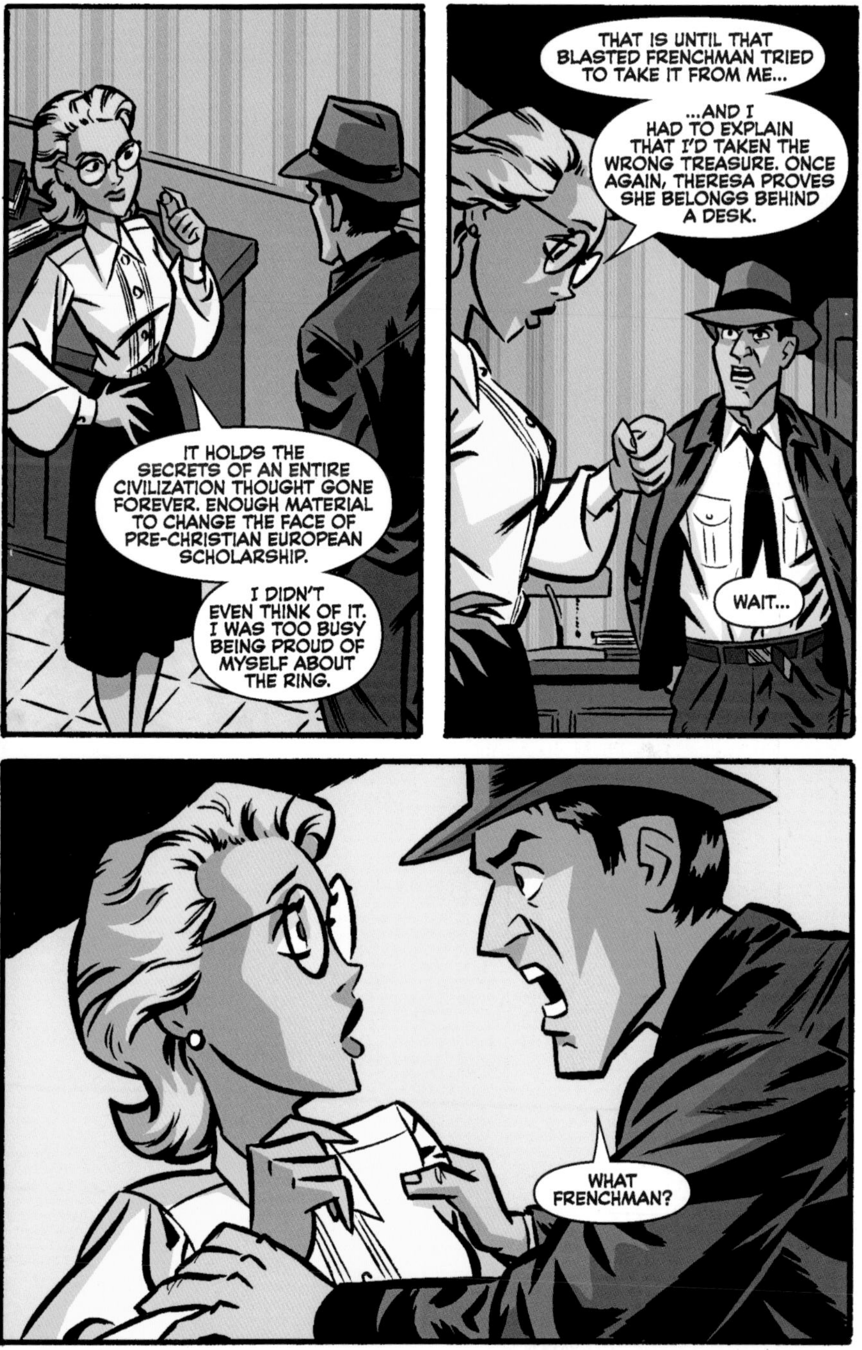
IT HOLDS THE SECRETS OF AN ENTIRE CIVILIZATION THOUGHT GONE FOREVER. ENOUGH MATERIAL TO CHANGE THE FACE OF PRE-CHRISTIAN EUROPEAN SCHOLARSHIP.
I DIDN'T EVEN THINK OF IT. I WAS TOO BUSY BEING PROUD OF MYSELF ABOUT THE RING.
THAT IS UNTIL THAT BLASTED FRENCHMAN TRIED TO TAKE IT FROM ME...
...AND I HAD TO EXPLAIN THAT I'D TAKEN THE WRONG TREASURE. ONCE AGAIN, THERESA PROVES SHE BELONGS BEHIND A DESK.
WAIT...
WHAT FRENCHMAN?

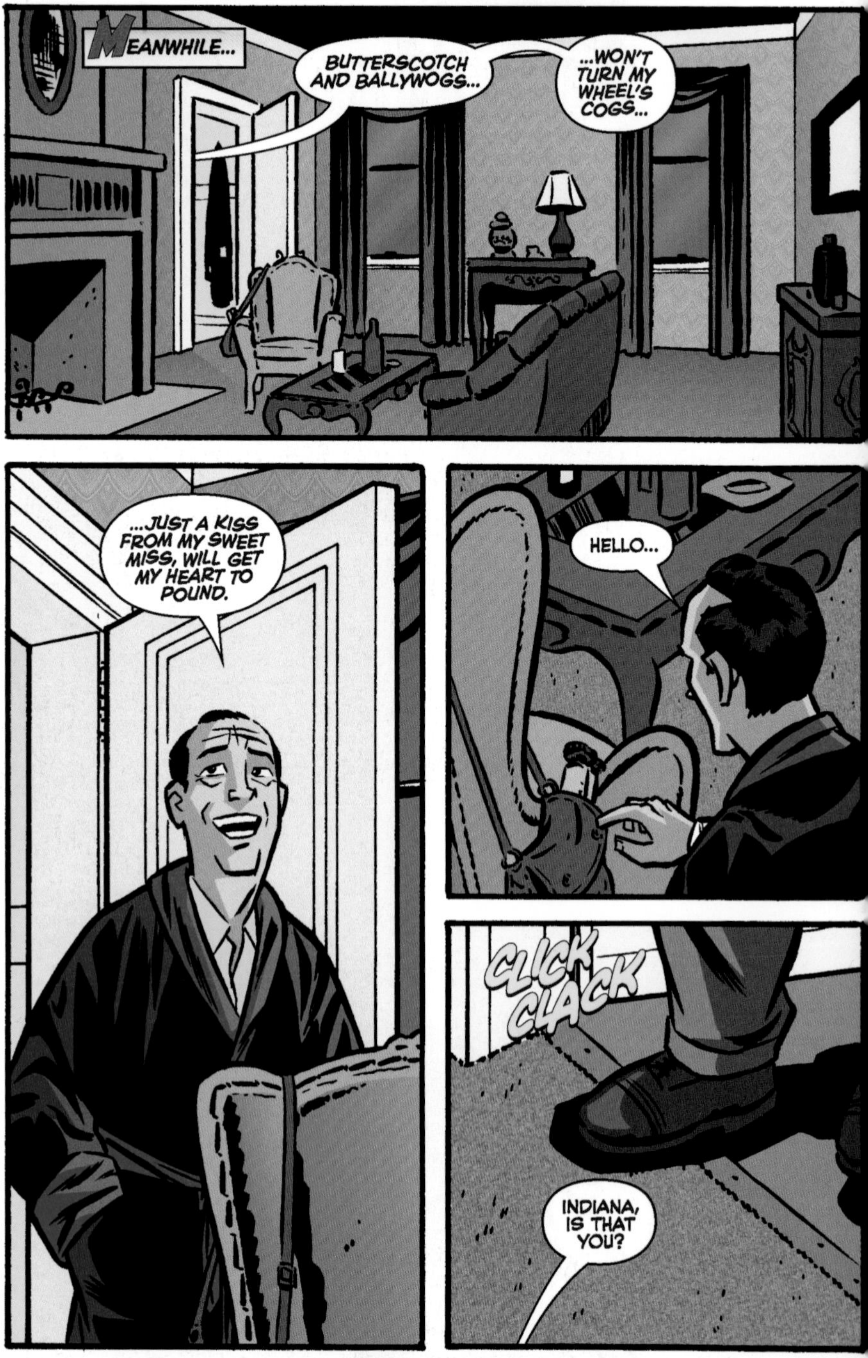
MEANWHILE...
BUTTERSCOTCH AND BALLYWOGS...
...WON'T TURN MY WHEEL'S COGS...
...JUST A KISS FROM MY SWEET MISS, WILL GET MY HEART TO POUND.
HELLO...
CLICK CLACK
INDIANA, IS THAT YOU?

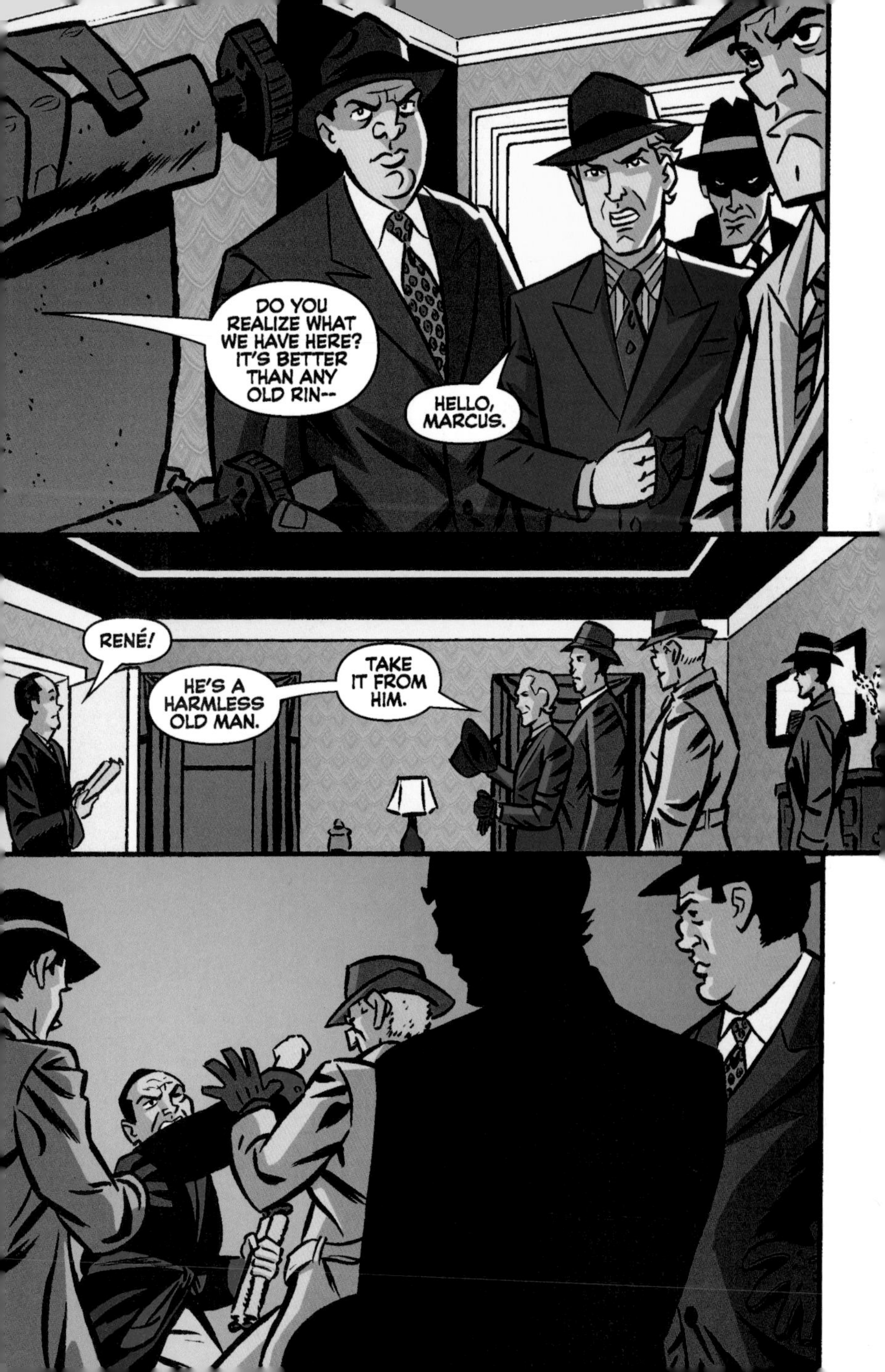
DO YOU REALIZE WHAT WE HAVE HERE? IT'S BETTER THAN ANY OLD RIN--
HELLO, MARCUS.
RENÉ!
HE'S A HARMLESS OLD MAN.
TAKE IT FROM HIM.

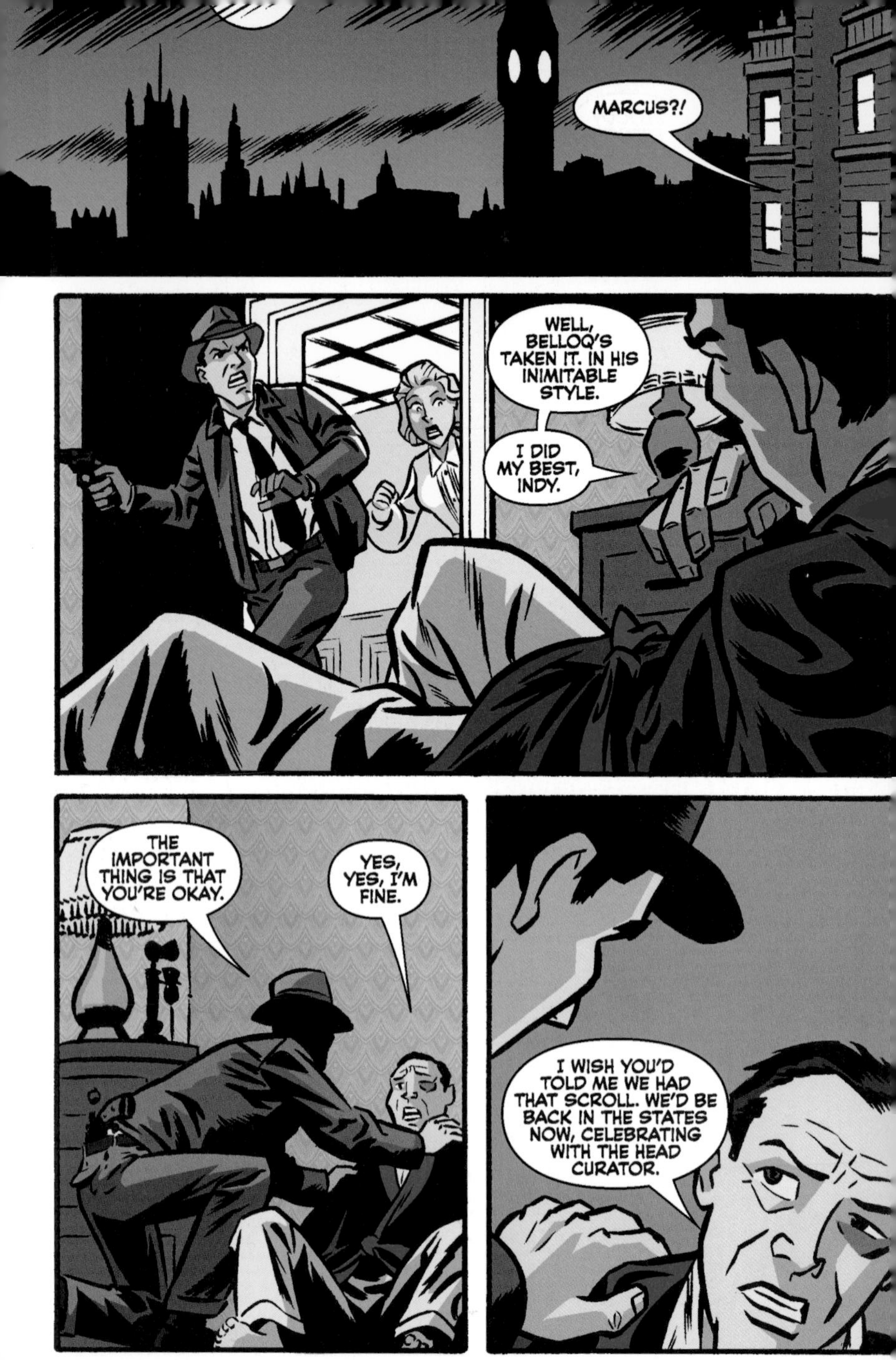
MARCUS?!
WELL, BELLOQ'S TAKEN IT. IN HIS INIMITABLE STYLE.
I DID MY BEST, INDY.
THE IMPORTANT THING IS THAT YOU'RE OKAY.
YES, YES, I'M FINE.
I WISH YOU'D TOLD ME WE HAD THAT SCROLL. WE'D BE BACK IN THE STATES NOW, CELEBRATING WITH THE HEAD CURATOR.

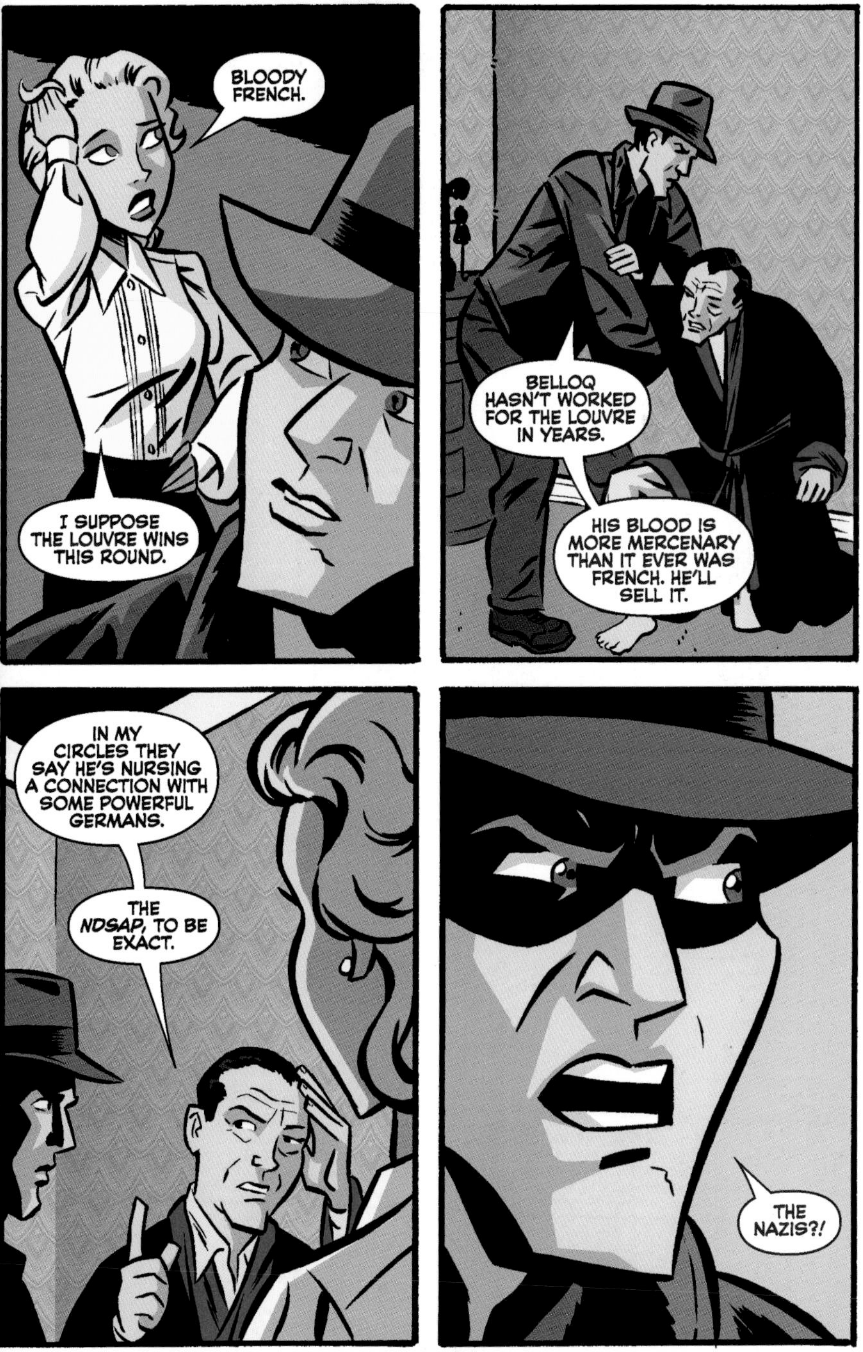
BLOODY FRENCH.
I SUPPOSE THE LOUVRE WINS THIS ROUND.
BELLOQ HASN'T WORKED FOR THE LOUVRE IN YEARS.
HIS BLOOD IS MORE MERCENARY THAN IT EVER WAS FRENCH. HE'LL SELL IT.
IN MY CIRCLES THEY SAY HE'S NURSING A CONNECTION WITH SOME POWERFUL GERMANS.
THE *NDSAP*, TO BE EXACT.
THE NAZIS?!

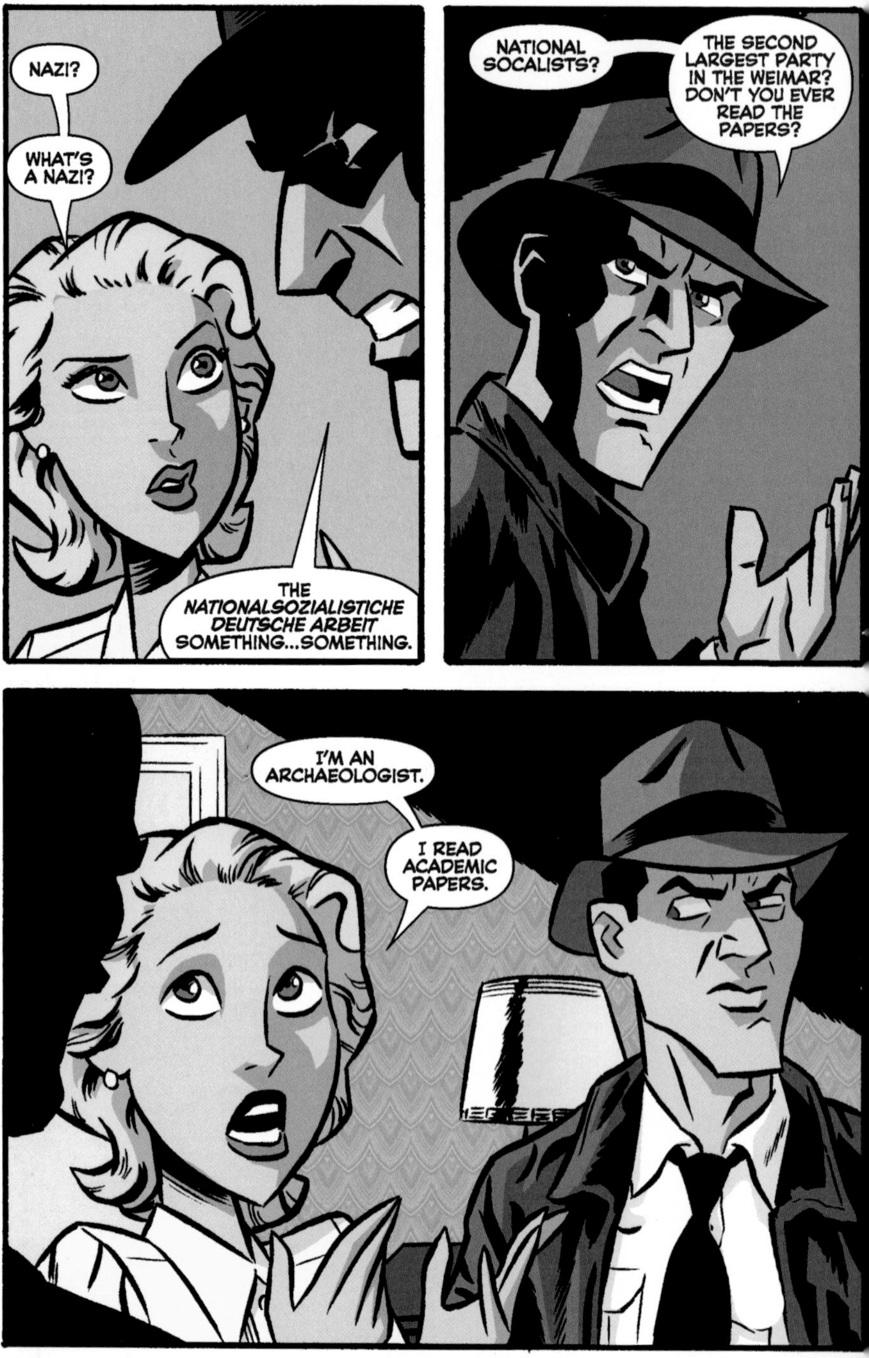
NAZI?
WHAT'S A NAZI?
THE *NATIONALSOZIALISTICHE DEUTSCHE ARBEIT* SOMETHING...SOMETHING.
NATIONAL SOCALISTS?
THE SECOND LARGEST PARTY IN THE WEIMAR? DON'T YOU EVER READ THE PAPERS?
I'M AN ARCHAEOLOGIST.
I READ ACADEMIC PAPERS.

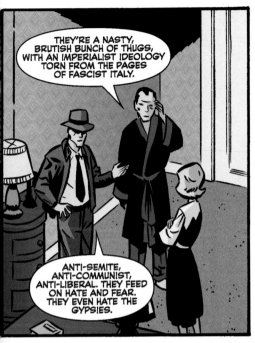

THEY'RE A NASTY, BRUTISH BUNCH OF THUGS, WITH AN IMPERIALIST IDEOLOGY TORN FROM THE PAGES OF FASCIST ITALY.

ANTI-SEMITE, ANTI-COMMUNIST, ANTI-LIBERAL. THEY FEED ON HATE AND FEAR. THEY EVEN HATE THE GYPSIES.

OH. OH, DEAR.

YOU SAID IT.

YOU THINK HE'D SELL TO THEM?

IF ANYONE COULD FIND THE APPEAL IN WORKING FOR SUCH APPALLING COLLECTORS, IT'D BE BELLOQ.

WE COULD GO TO THE AUTHORITIES, BUT HE'LL GET IT OUT OF THE COUNTRY AS SOON AS POSSIBLE. TAKE IT SOMEWHERE WHERE EUROPEAN LAW CAN'T CATCH HIM IN THE ACT.

EXCUSE US FOR A MOMENT, DR. LAWRENCE.

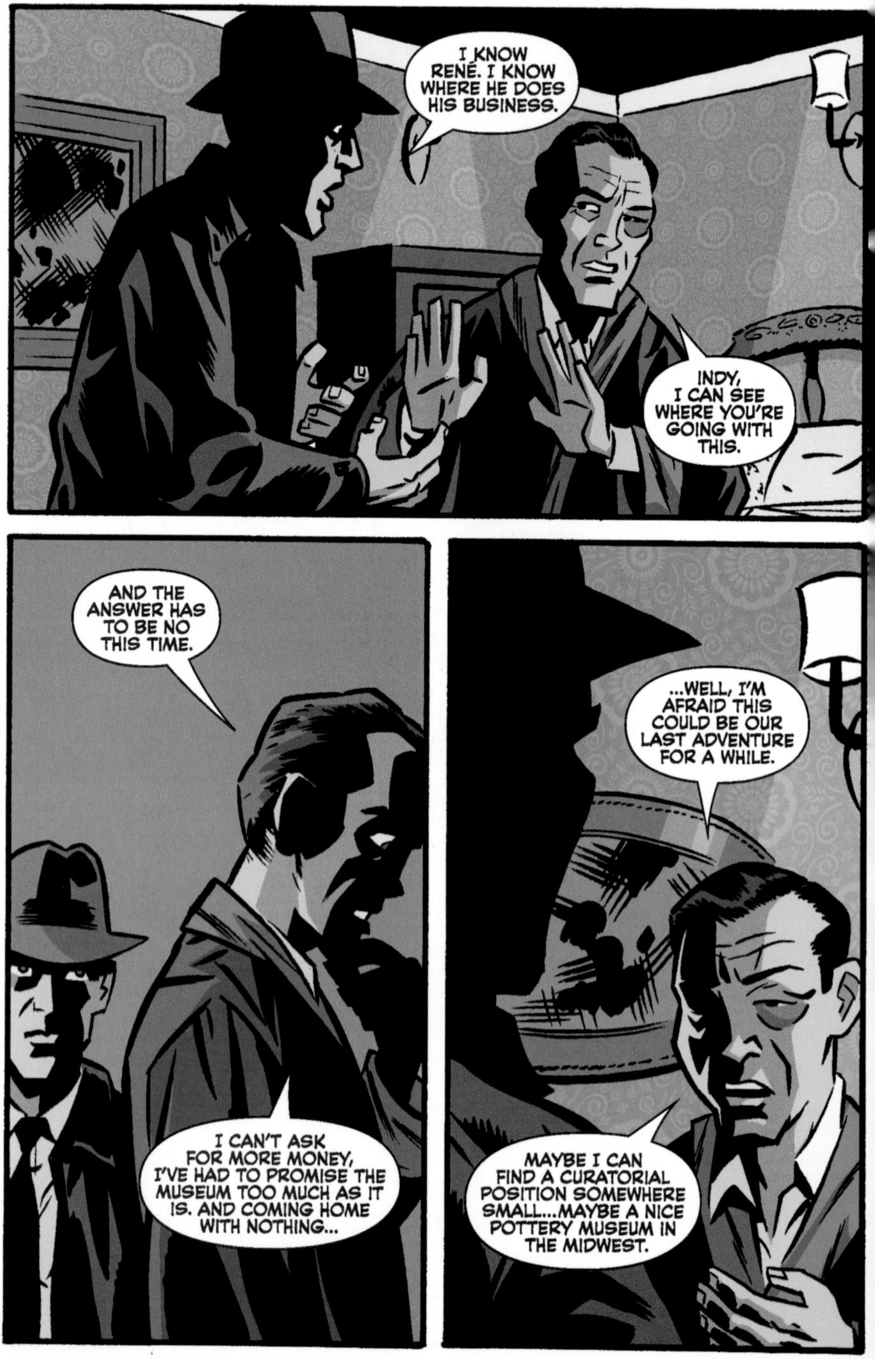
I KNOW RENÉ. I KNOW WHERE HE DOES HIS BUSINESS.
INDY, I CAN SEE WHERE YOU'RE GOING WITH THIS.
AND THE ANSWER HAS TO BE NO THIS TIME.
I CAN'T ASK FOR MORE MONEY, I'VE HAD TO PROMISE THE MUSEUM TOO MUCH AS IT IS. AND COMING HOME WITH NOTHING...
...WELL, I'M AFRAID THIS COULD BE OUR LAST ADVENTURE FOR A WHILE.
MAYBE I CAN FIND A CURATORIAL POSITION SOMEWHERE SMALL...MAYBE A NICE POTTERY MUSEUM IN THE MIDWEST.

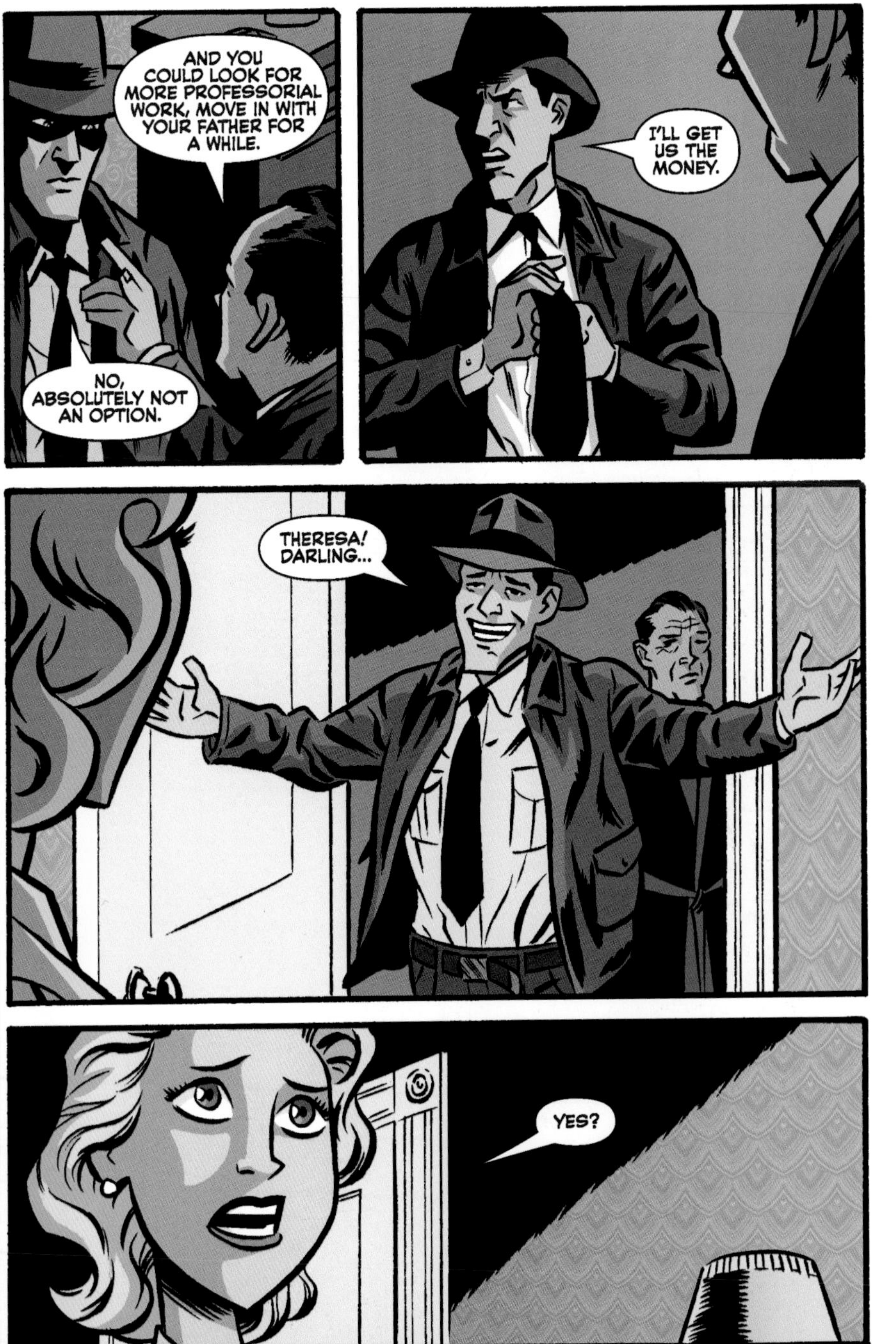
AND YOU COULD LOOK FOR MORE PROFESSORIAL WORK, MOVE IN WITH YOUR FATHER FOR A WHILE.
NO, ABSOLUTELY NOT AN OPTION.
I'LL GET US THE MONEY.
THERESA! DARLING...
YES?

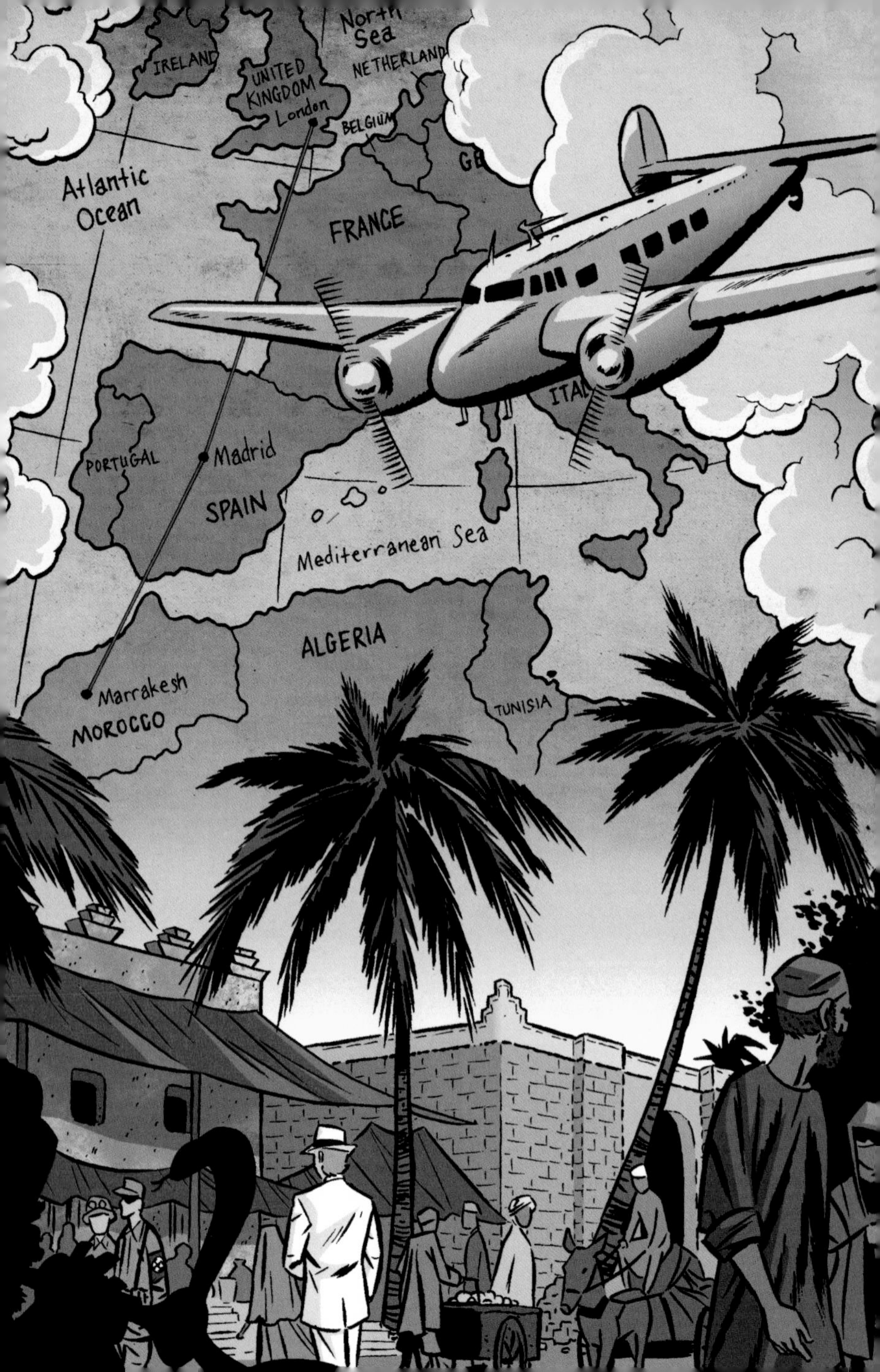
North Sea
IRELAND
UNITED KINGDOM
London
NETHERLAND
BELGIUM
Atlantic Ocean
FRANCE
PORTUGAL
Madrid
SPAIN
Mediterranean Sea
ALGERIA
Marrakesh
MOROCCO
TUNISIA

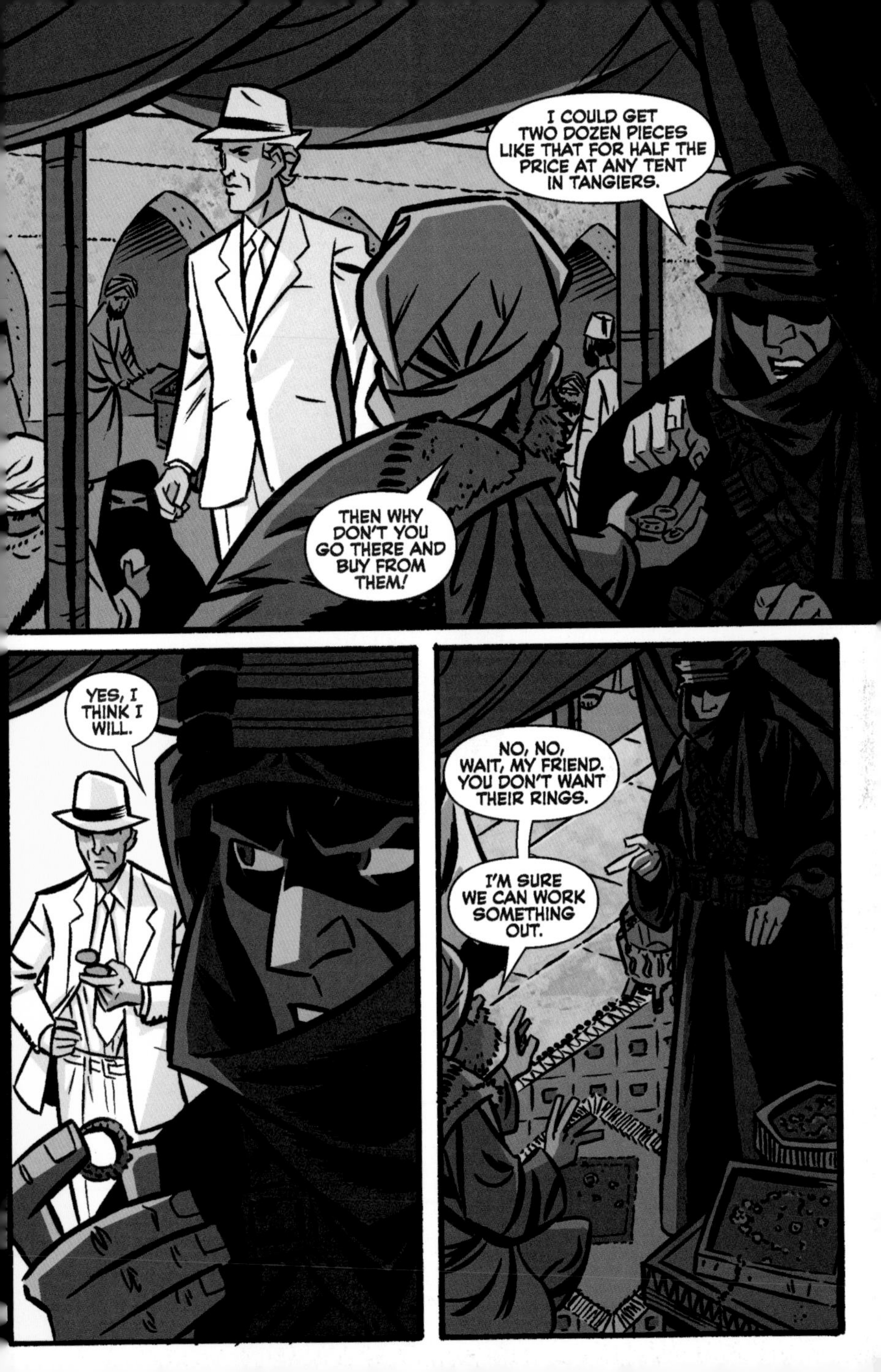
I COULD GET TWO DOZEN PIECES LIKE THAT FOR HALF THE PRICE AT ANY TENT IN TANGIERS.
THEN WHY DON'T YOU GO THERE AND BUY FROM THEM!
YES, I THINK I WILL.
NO, NO, WAIT, MY FRIEND. YOU DON'T WANT THEIR RINGS.
I'M SURE WE CAN WORK SOMETHING OUT.

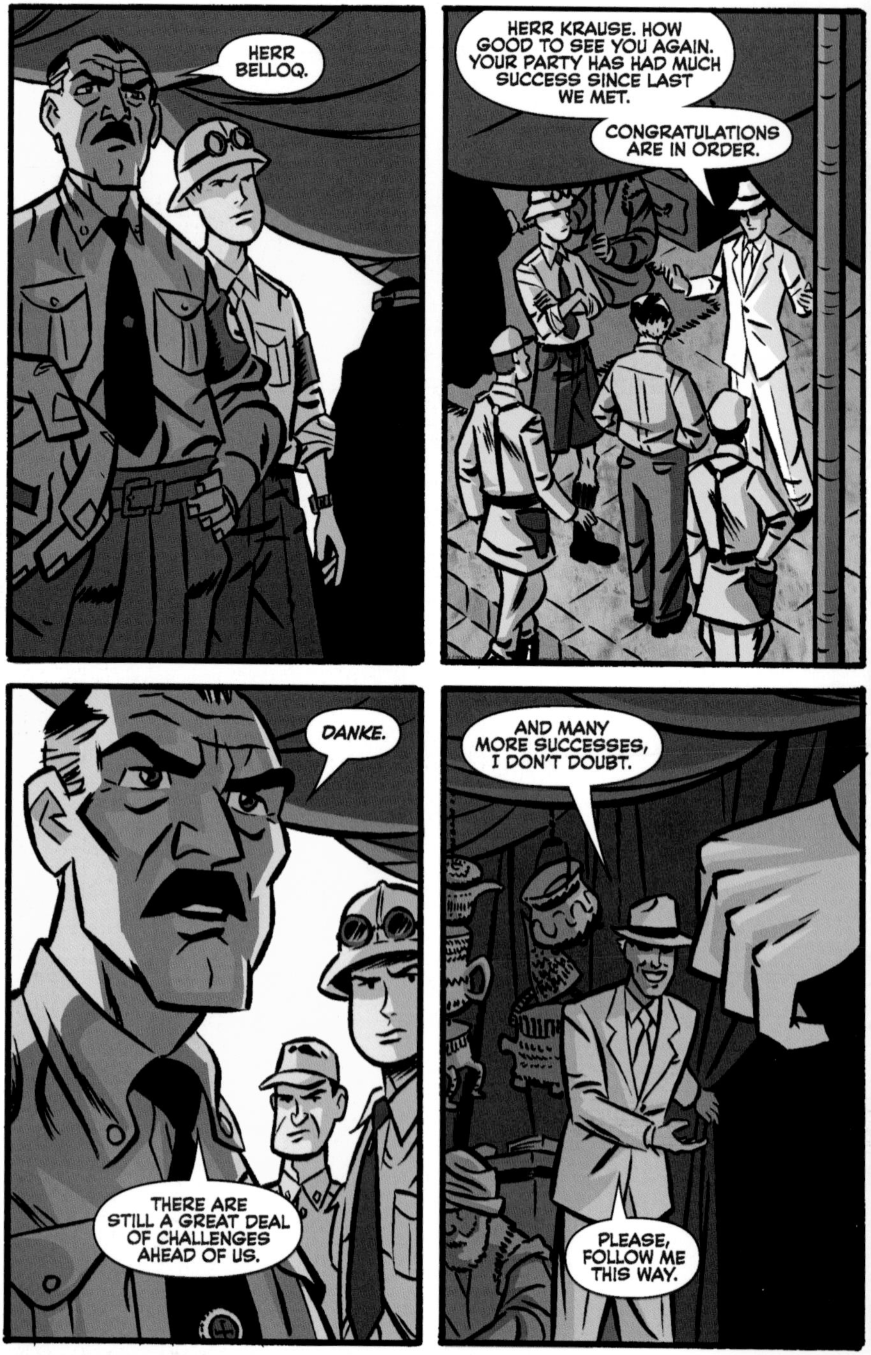
HERR BELLOQ.
HERR KRAUSE. HOW GOOD TO SEE YOU AGAIN. YOUR PARTY HAS HAD MUCH SUCCESS SINCE LAST WE MET.
CONGRATULATIONS ARE IN ORDER.
DANKE.
THERE ARE STILL A GREAT DEAL OF CHALLENGES AHEAD OF US.
AND MANY MORE SUCCESSES, I DON'T DOUBT.
PLEASE, FOLLOW ME THIS WAY.

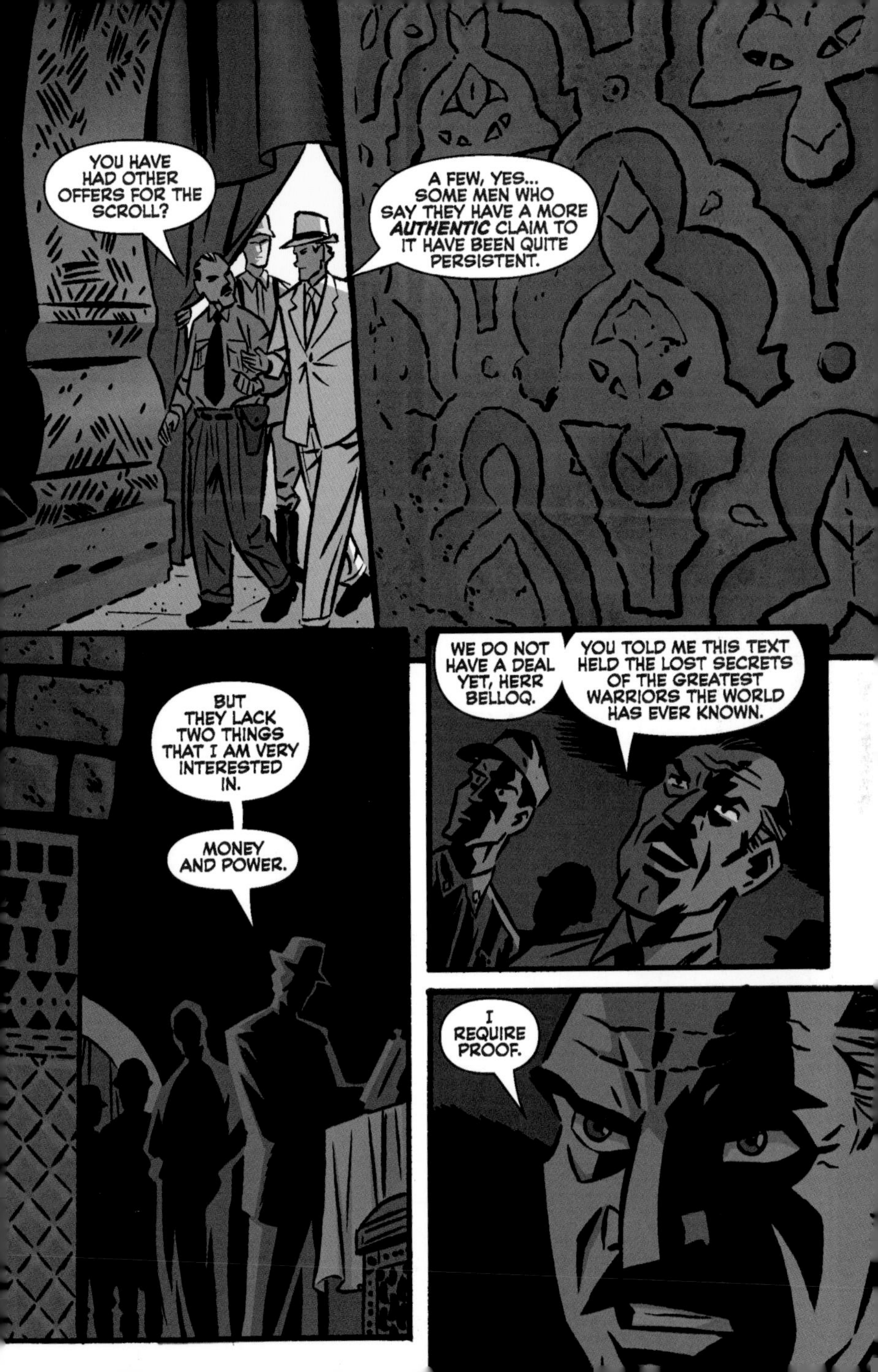
YOU HAVE HAD OTHER OFFERS FOR THE SCROLL?
A FEW, YES... SOME MEN WHO SAY THEY HAVE A MORE *AUTHENTIC* CLAIM TO IT HAVE BEEN QUITE PERSISTENT.
BUT THEY LACK TWO THINGS THAT I AM VERY INTERESTED IN.
MONEY AND POWER.
WE DO NOT HAVE A DEAL YET, HERR BELLOQ.
YOU TOLD ME THIS TEXT HELD THE LOST SECRETS OF THE GREATEST WARRIORS THE WORLD HAS EVER KNOWN.
I REQUIRE PROOF.

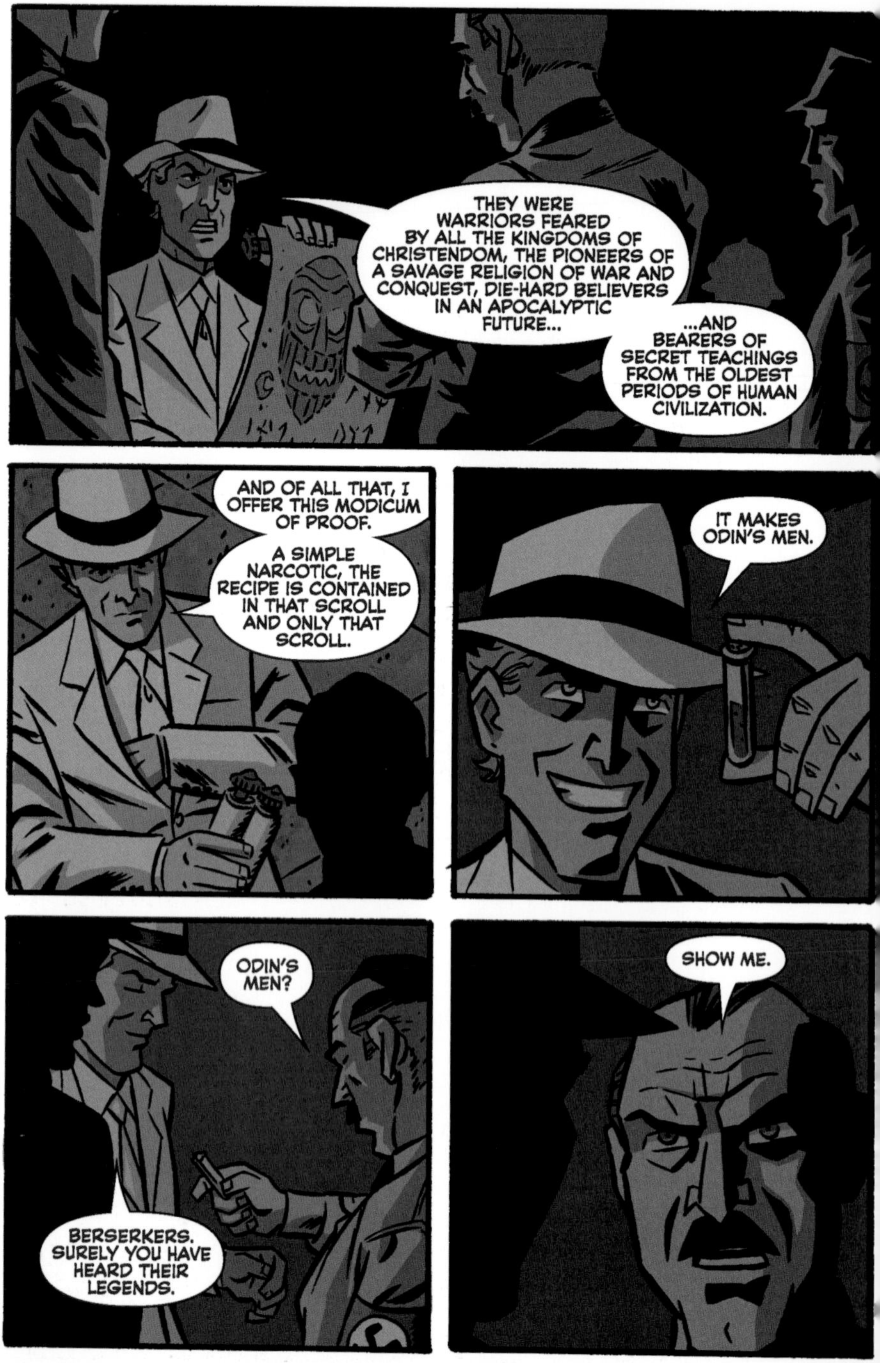
THEY WERE WARRIORS FEARED BY ALL THE KINGDOMS OF CHRISTENDOM, THE PIONEERS OF A SAVAGE RELIGION OF WAR AND CONQUEST, DIE-HARD BELIEVERS IN AN APOCALYPTIC FUTURE...
...AND BEARERS OF SECRET TEACHINGS FROM THE OLDEST PERIODS OF HUMAN CIVILIZATION.
AND OF ALL THAT, I OFFER THIS MODICUM OF PROOF.
A SIMPLE NARCOTIC, THE RECIPE IS CONTAINED IN THAT SCROLL AND ONLY THAT SCROLL.
IT MAKES ODIN'S MEN.
ODIN'S MEN?
BERSERKERS. SURELY YOU HAVE HEARD THEIR LEGENDS.
SHOW ME.

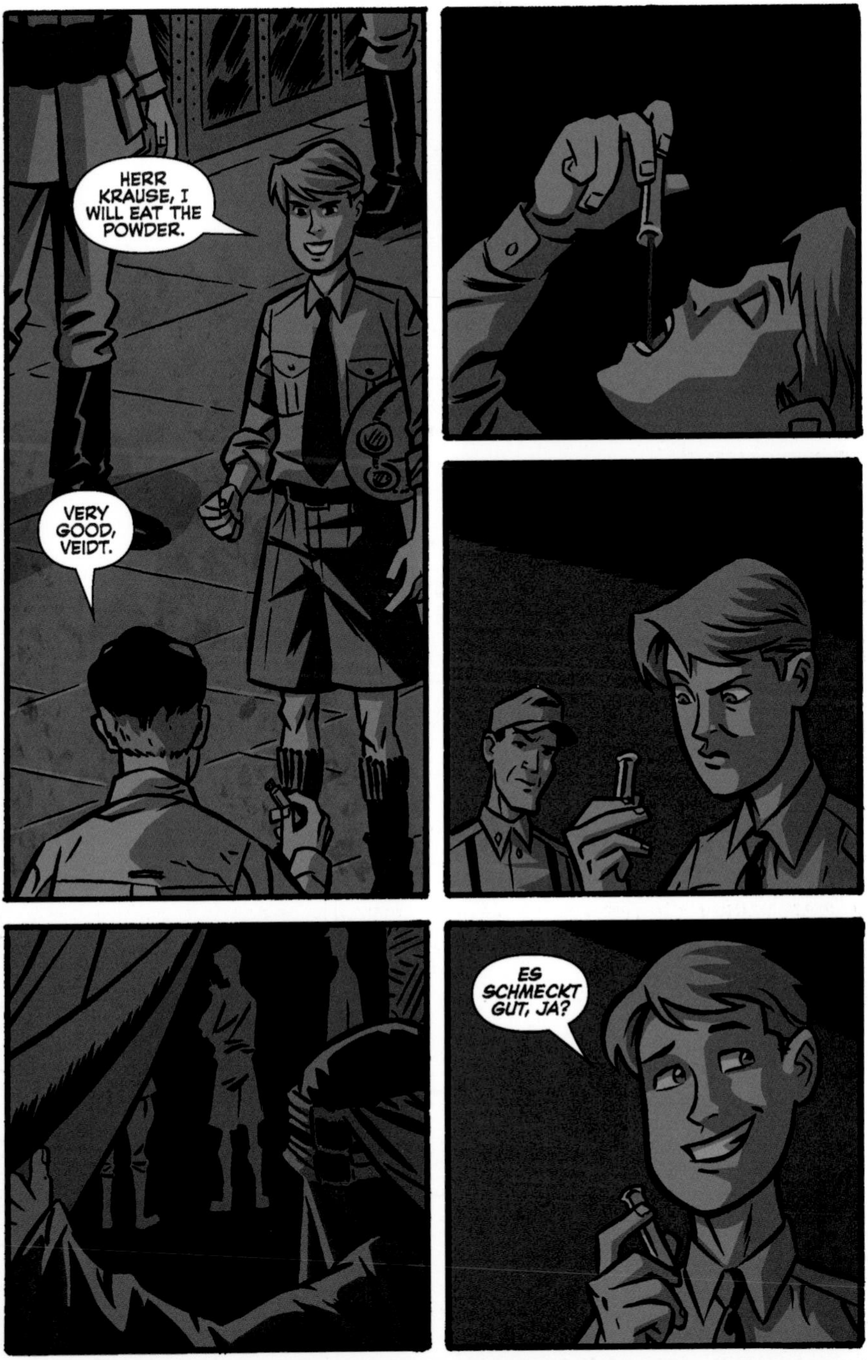
HERR KRAUSE, I WILL EAT THE POWDER.
VERY GOOD, VEIDT.
ES SCHMECKT GUT, JA?

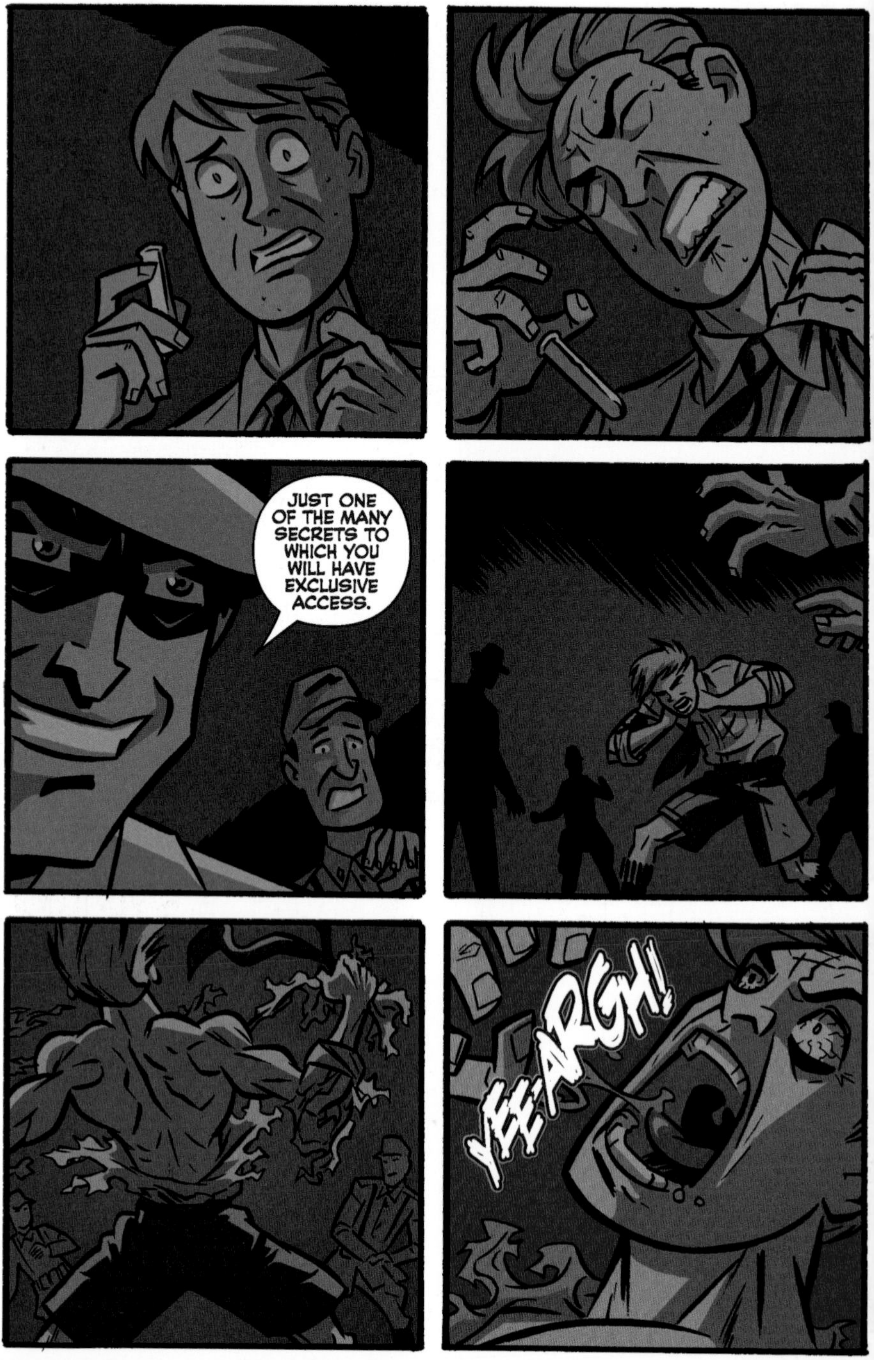
JUST ONE OF THE MANY SECRETS TO WHICH YOU WILL HAVE EXCLUSIVE ACCESS.
YEEARGH!

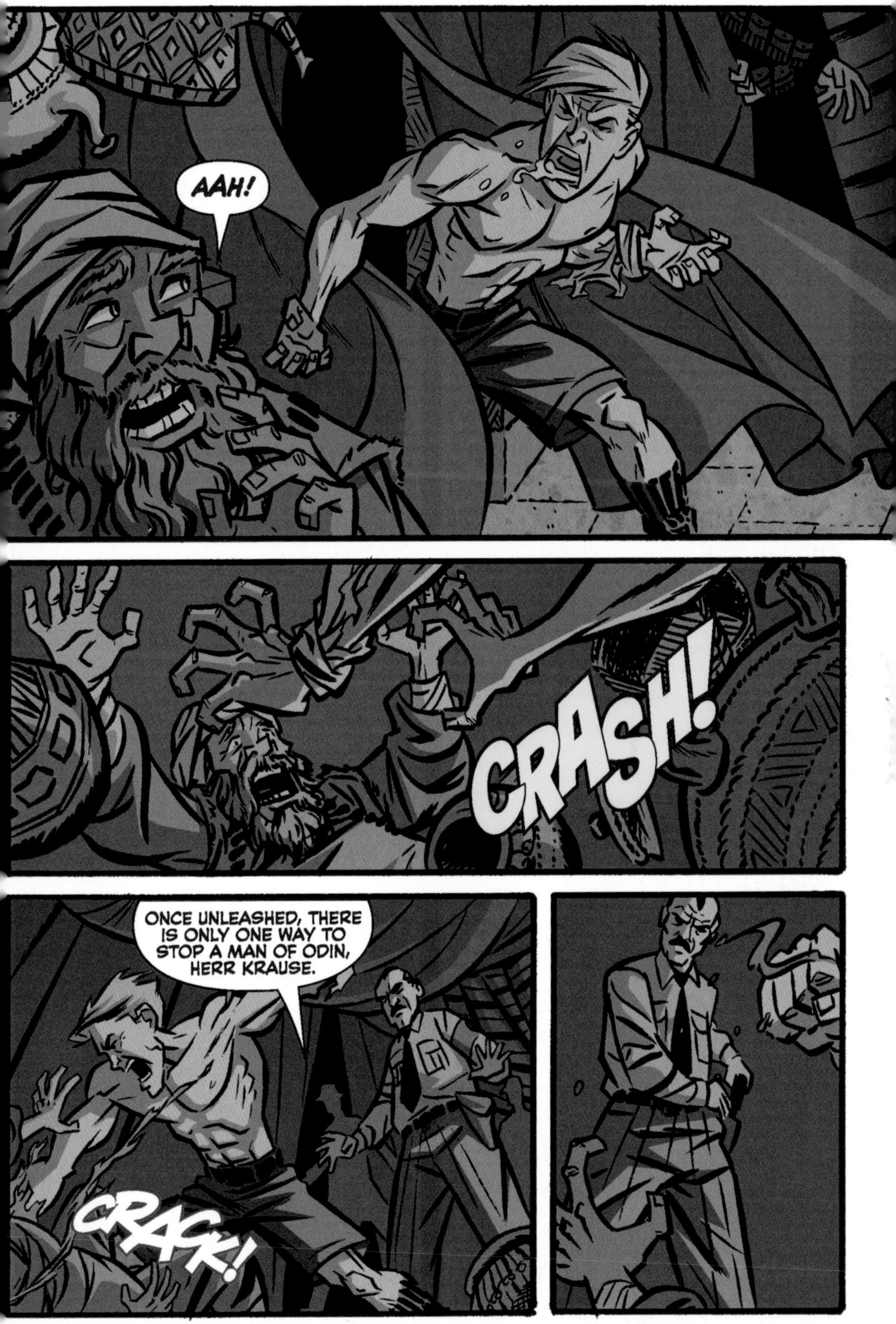
AAH!
CRASH!
ONCE UNLEASHED, THERE IS ONLY ONE WAY TO STOP A MAN OF ODIN, HERR KRAUSE.
CRACK!

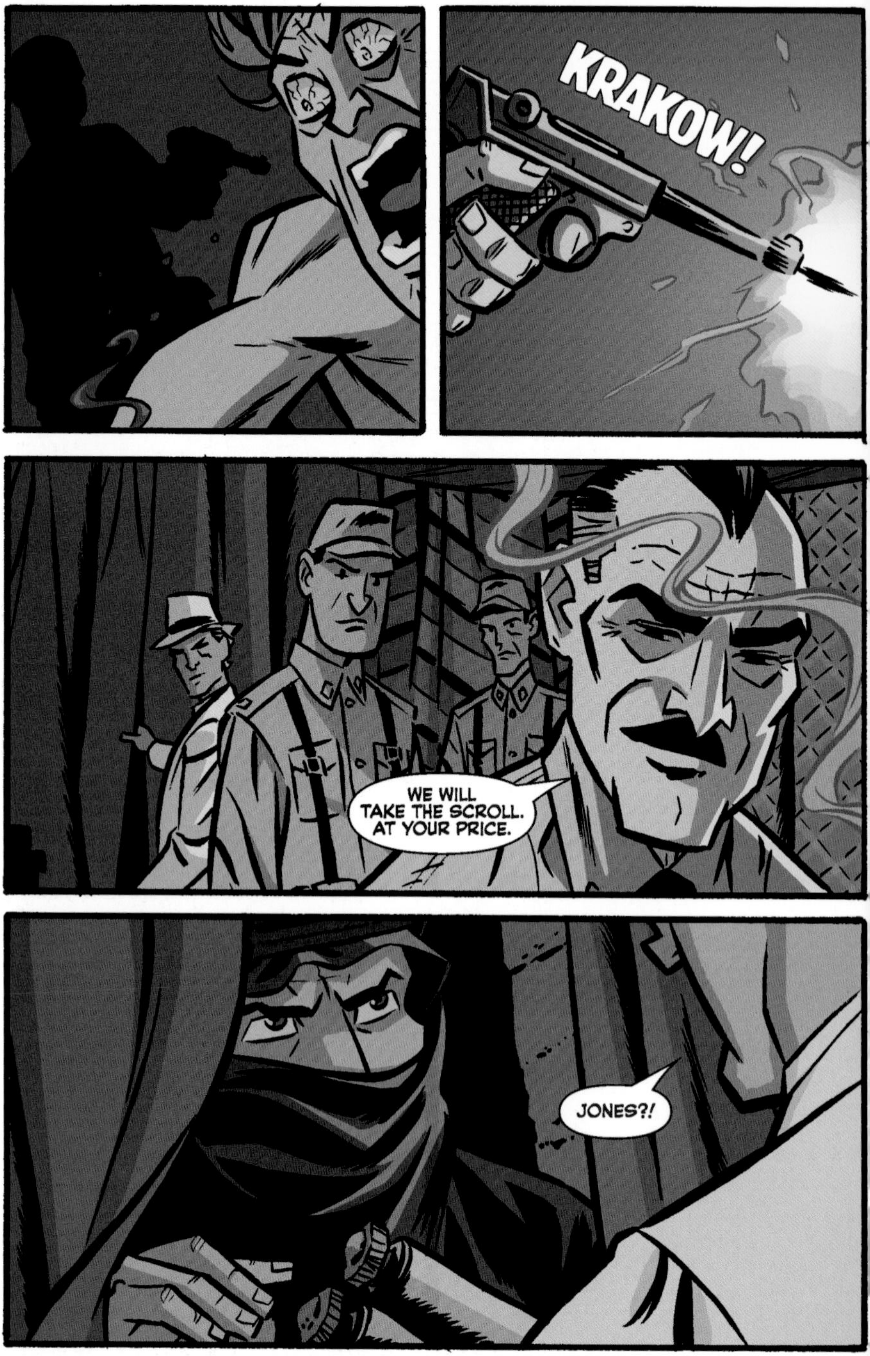
KRAKOW!
WE WILL TAKE THE SCROLL. AT YOUR PRICE.
JONES?!

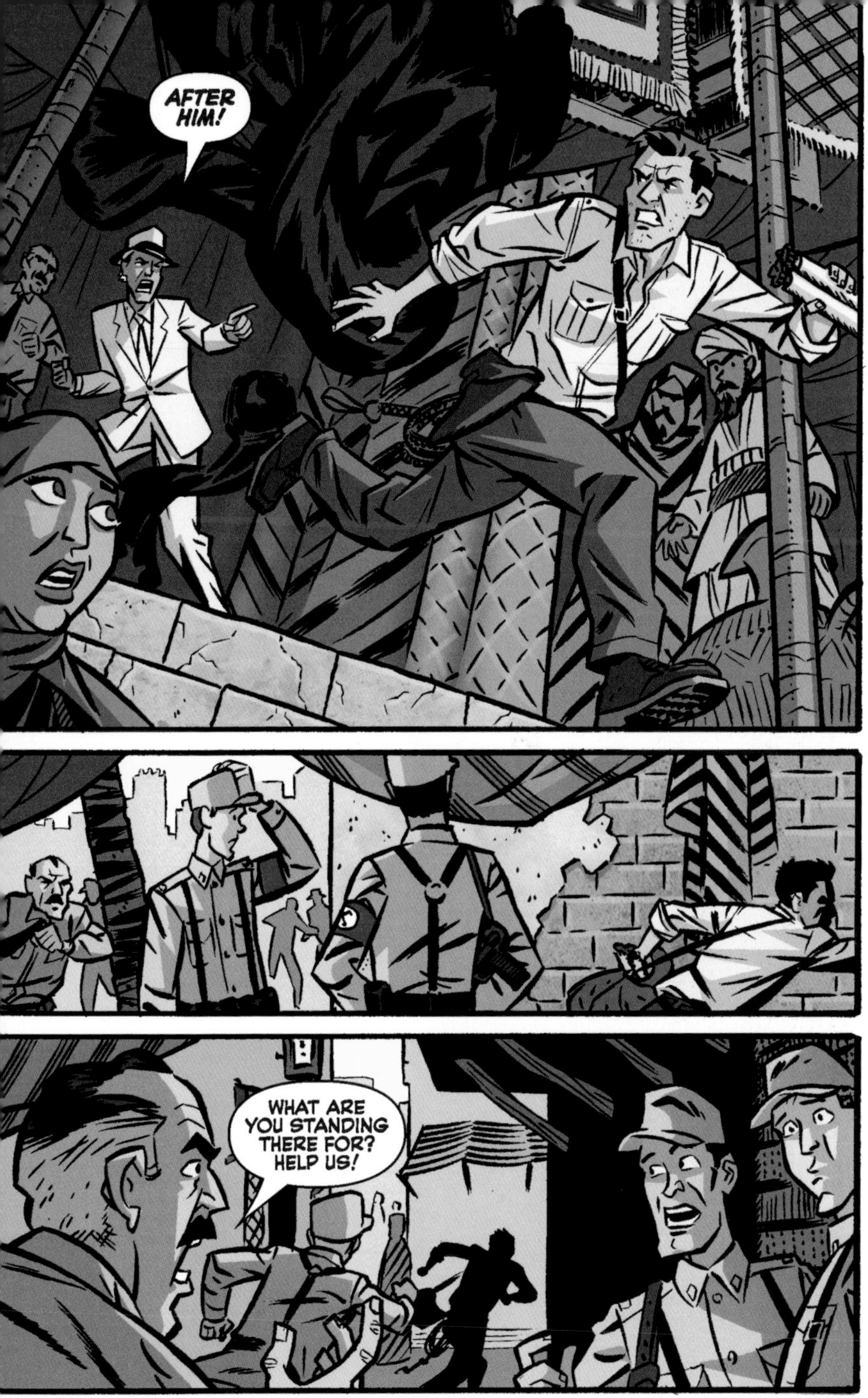
AFTER HIM!
WHAT ARE YOU STANDING THERE FOR? HELP US!

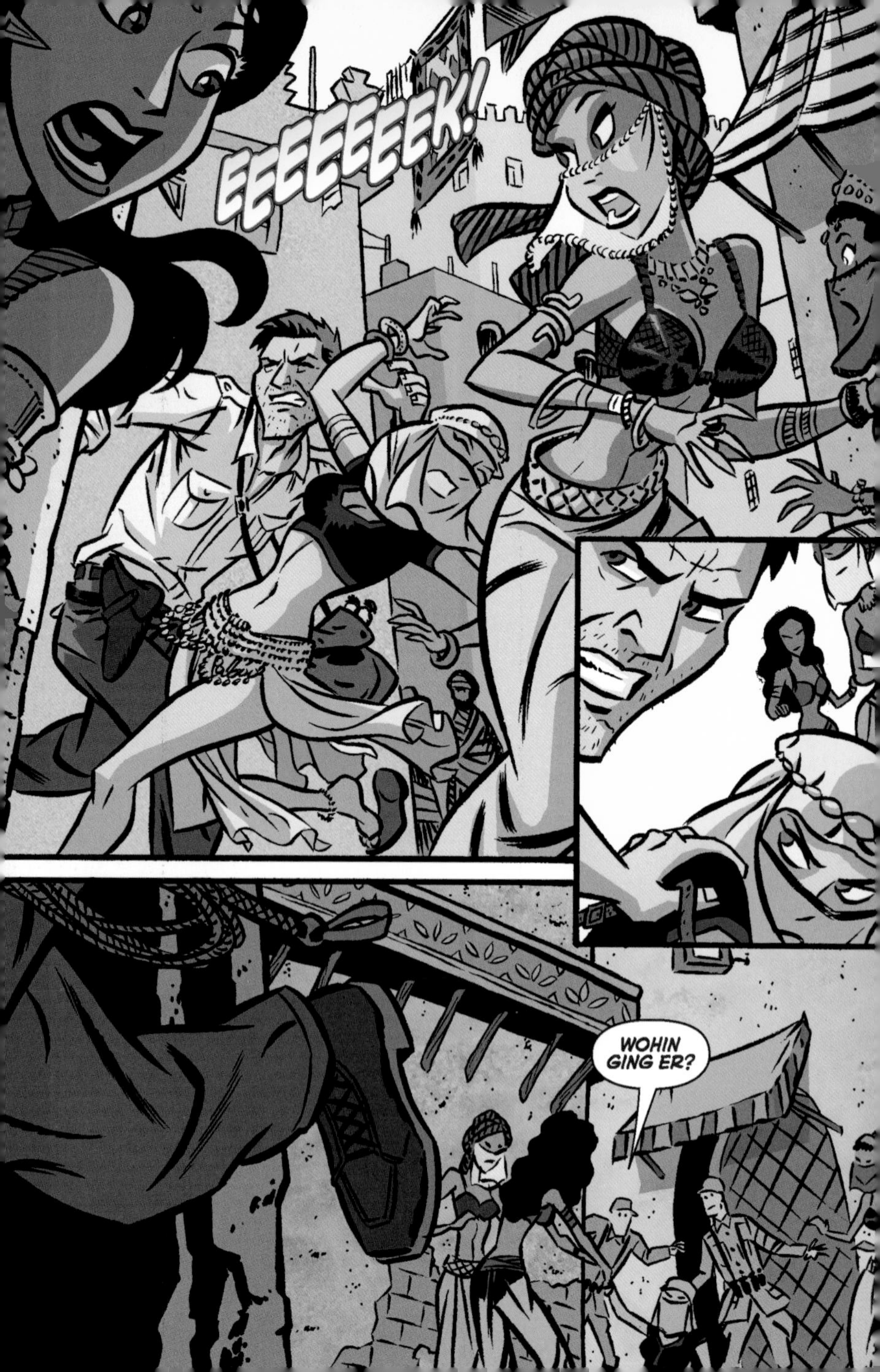
EEEEEEEEK!
WOHIN GING ER?

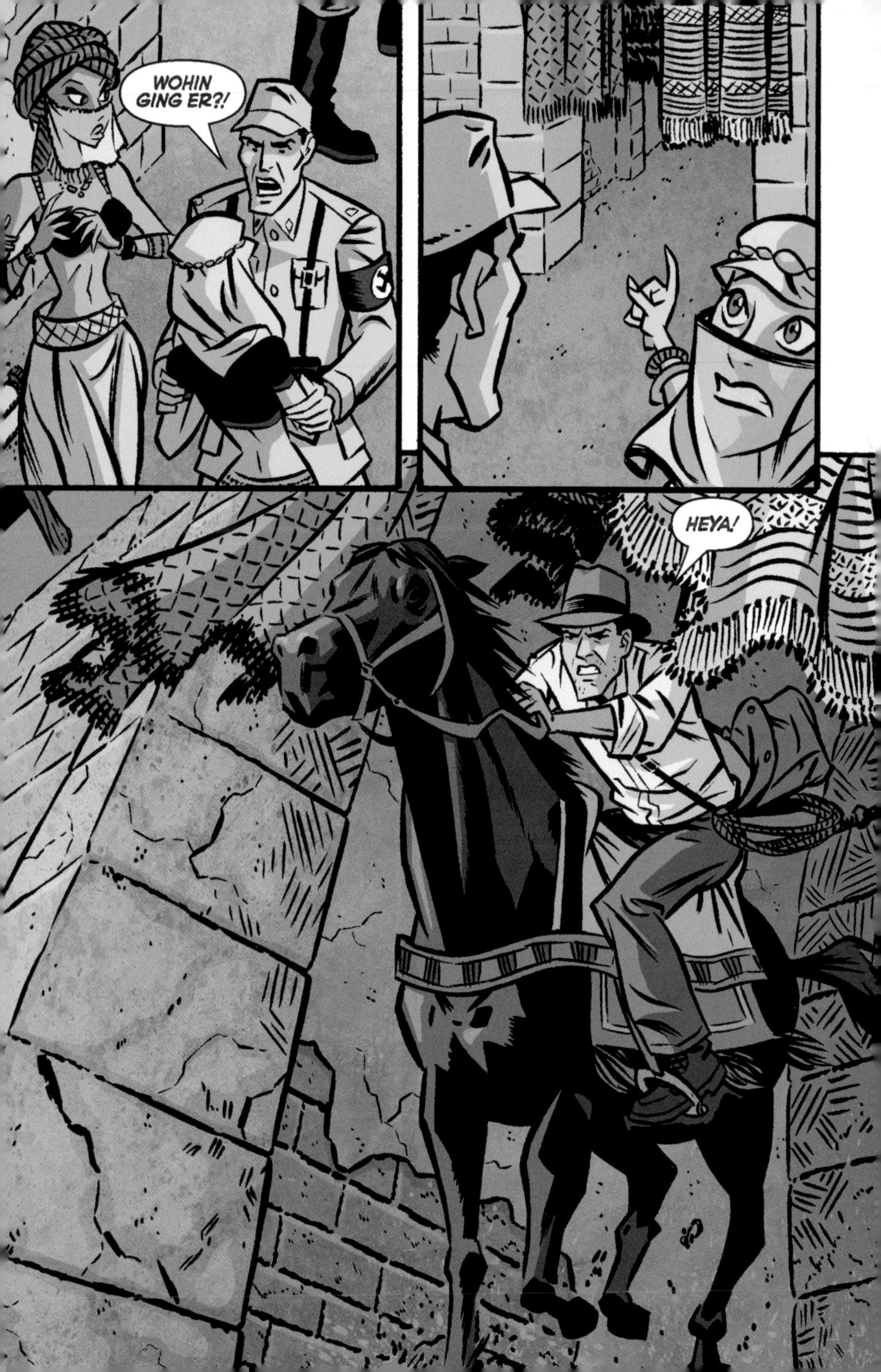
WOHIN GING ER?!
HEYA!

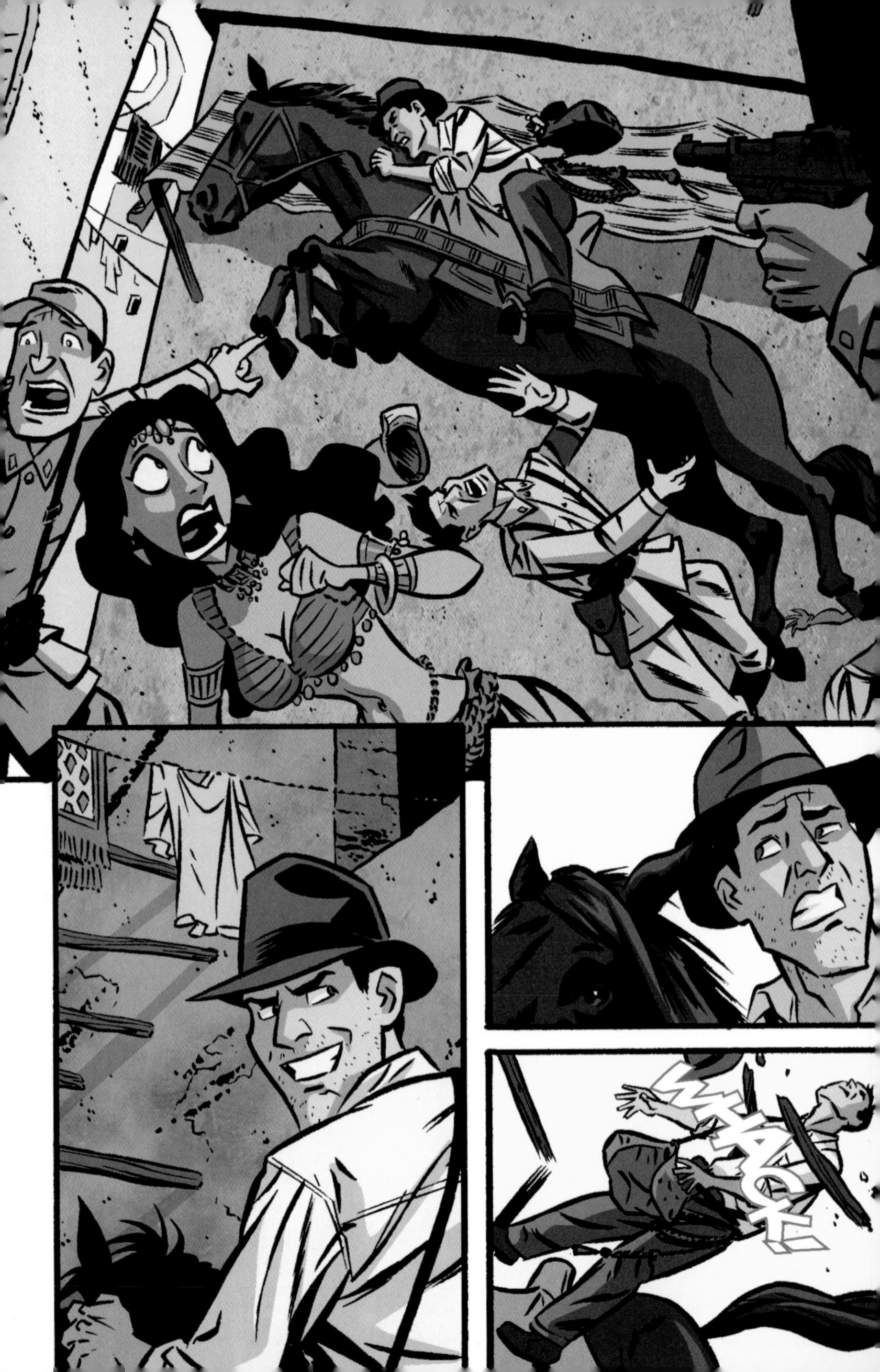
WHACK!

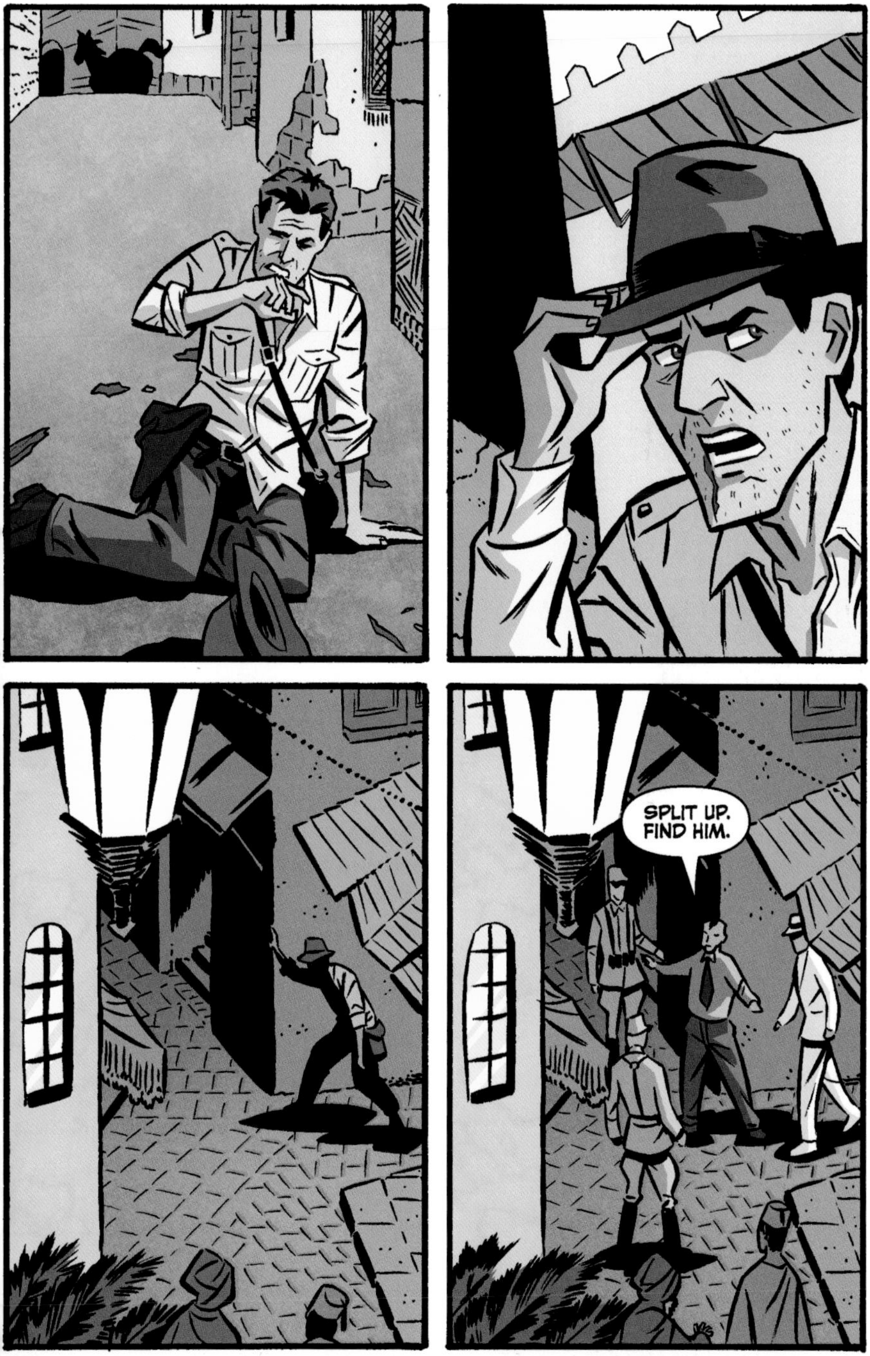
SPLIT UP.
FIND HIM.

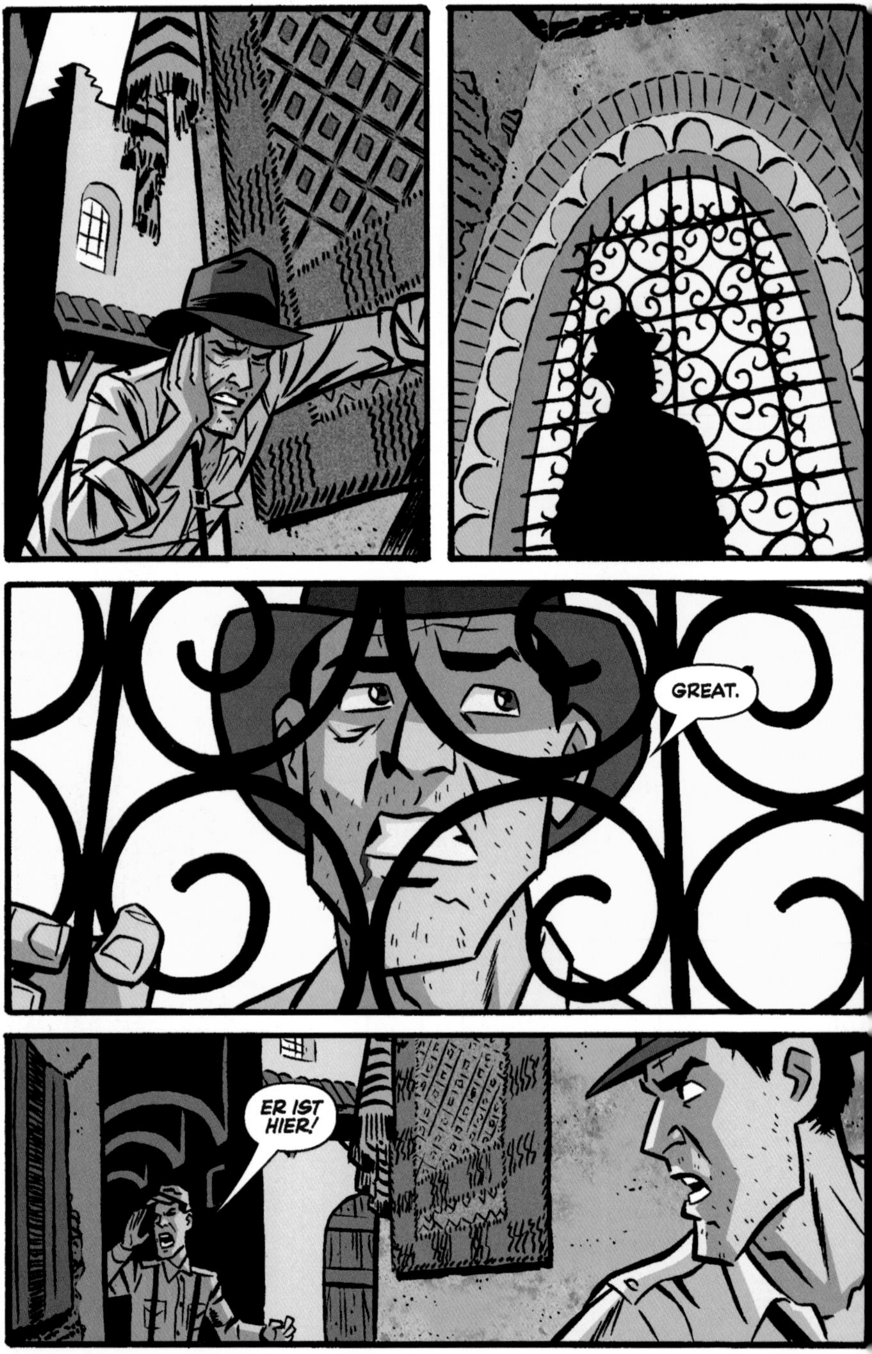
GREAT.
ER IST HIER!

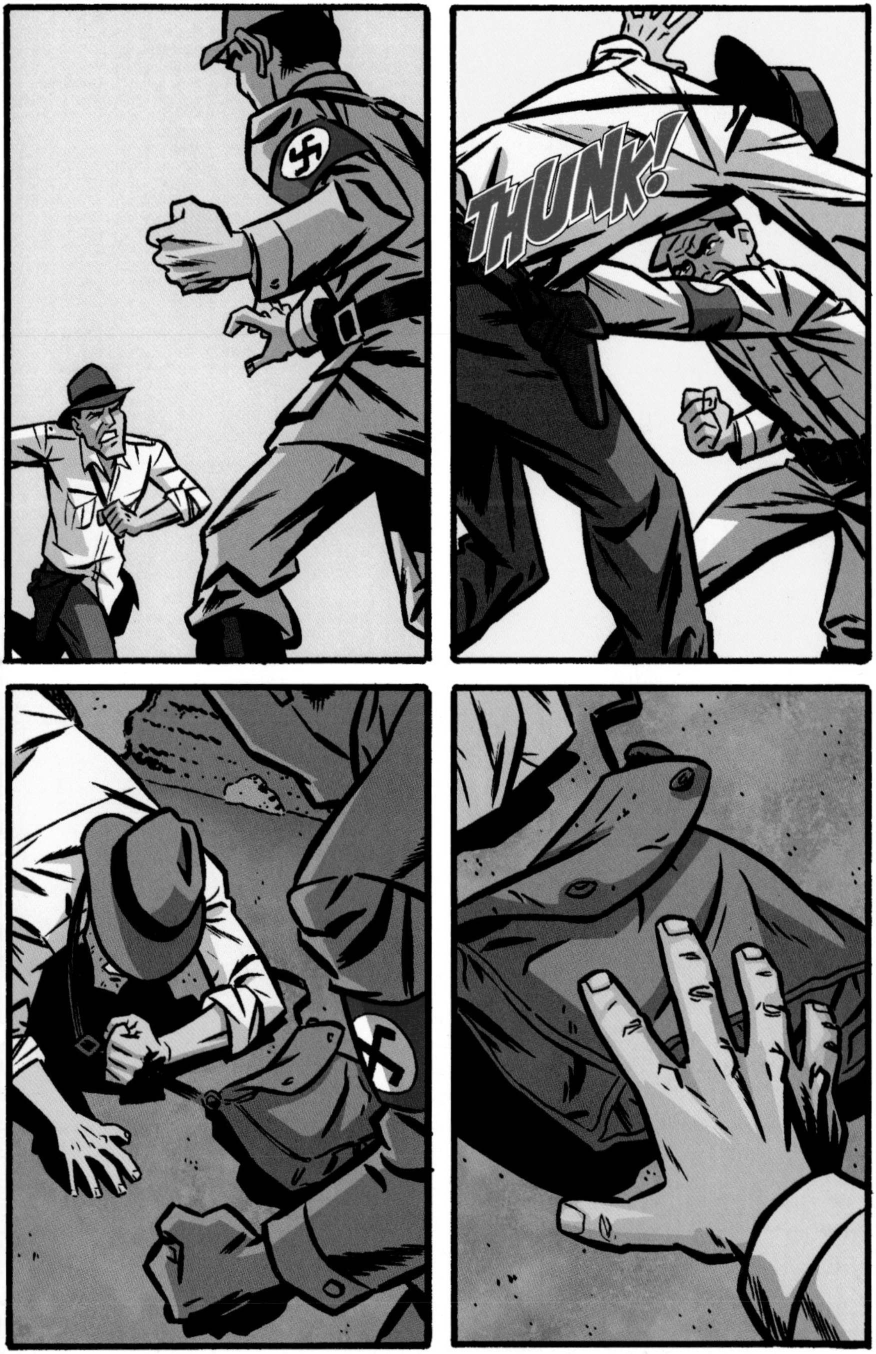
THUNK!

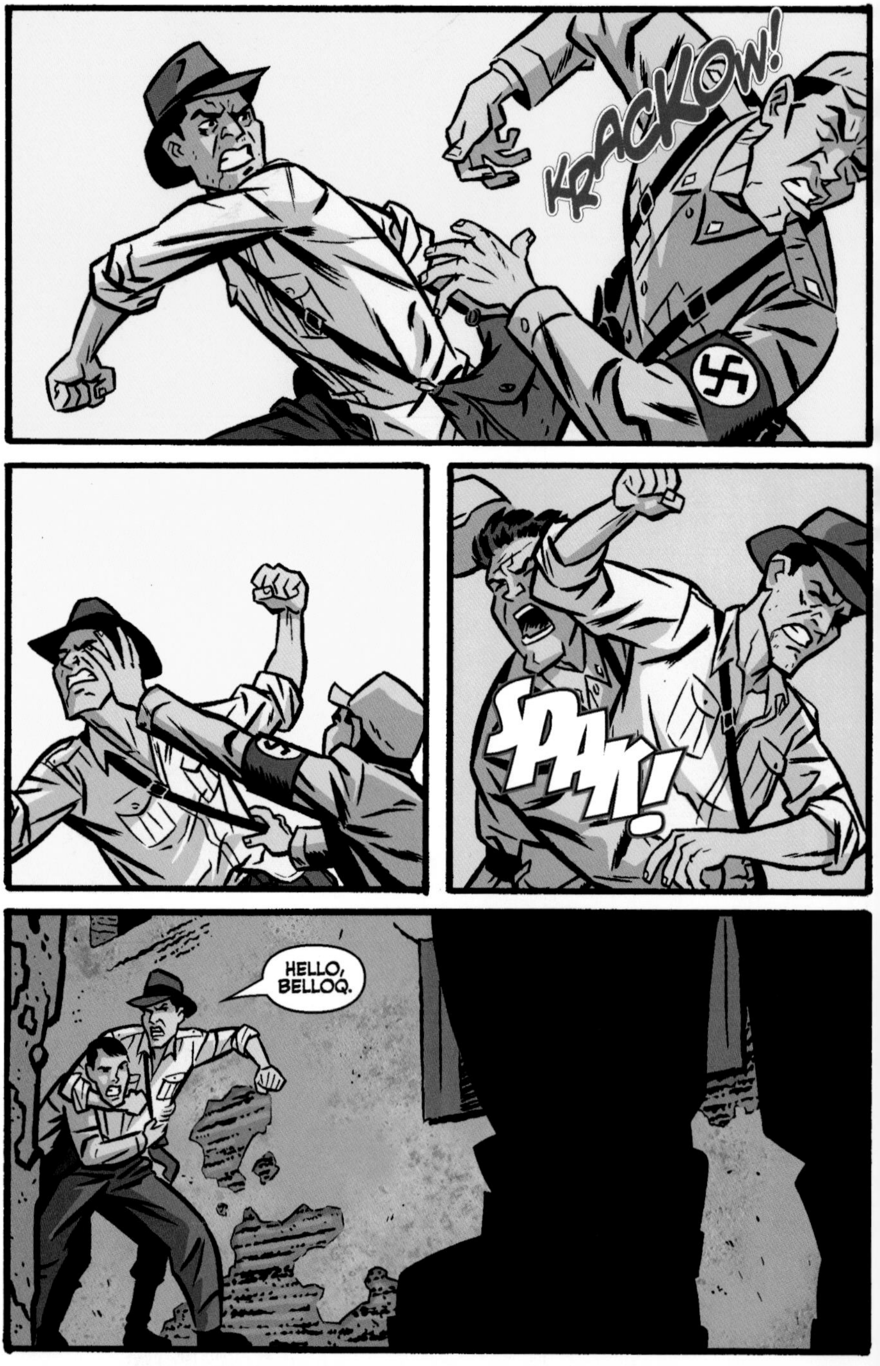
KRACKOW!
SPAK!
HELLO, BELLOQ.

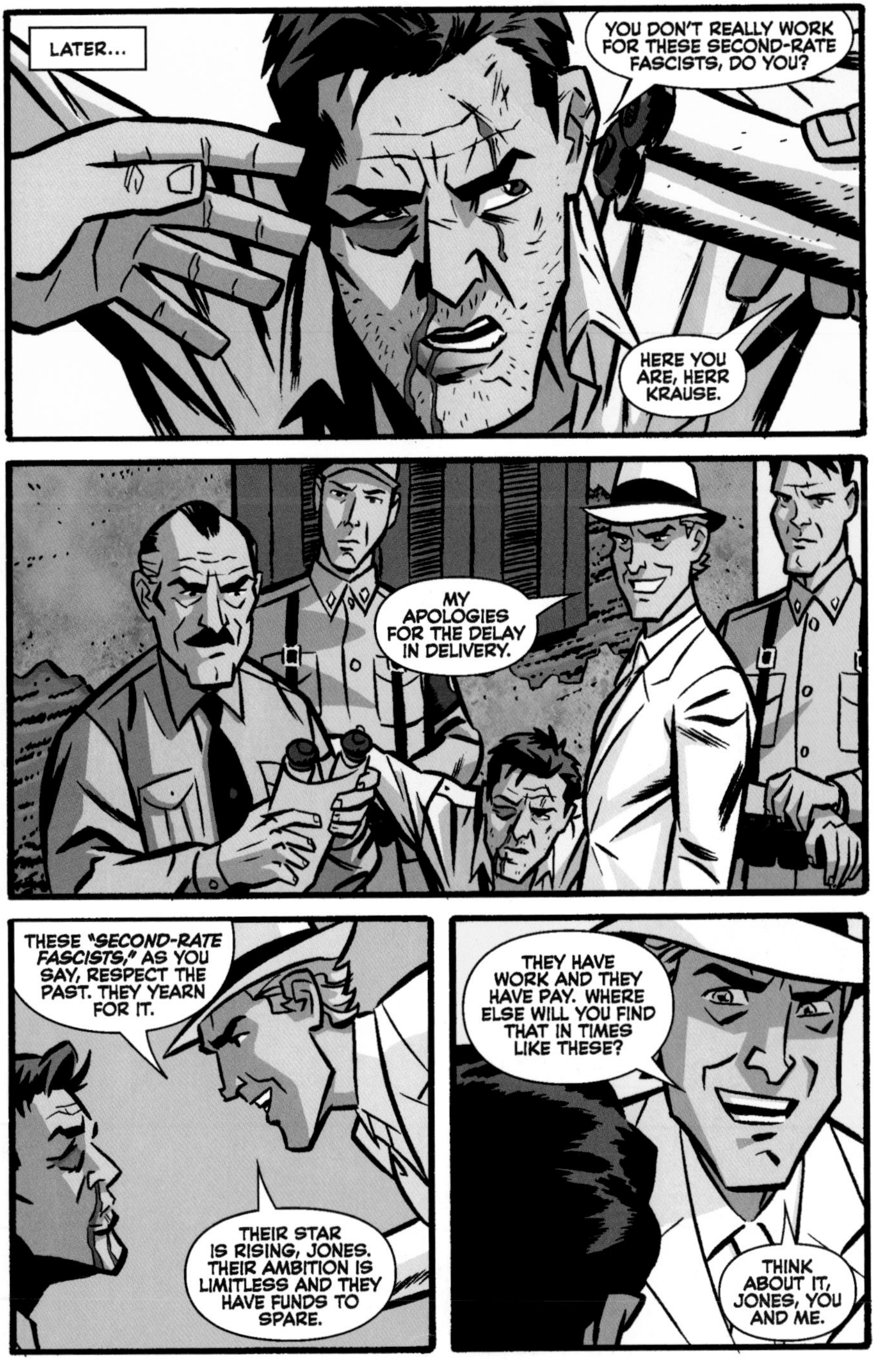
LATER...
YOU DON'T REALLY WORK FOR THESE SECOND-RATE FASCISTS, DO YOU?
HERE YOU ARE, HERR KRAUSE.
MY APOLOGIES FOR THE DELAY IN DELIVERY.
THESE "SECOND-RATE FASCISTS," AS YOU SAY, RESPECT THE PAST. THEY YEARN FOR IT.
THEIR STAR IS RISING, JONES. THEIR AMBITION IS LIMITLESS AND THEY HAVE FUNDS TO SPARE.
THEY HAVE WORK AND THEY HAVE PAY. WHERE ELSE WILL YOU FIND THAT IN TIMES LIKE THESE?
THINK ABOUT IT, JONES, YOU AND ME.

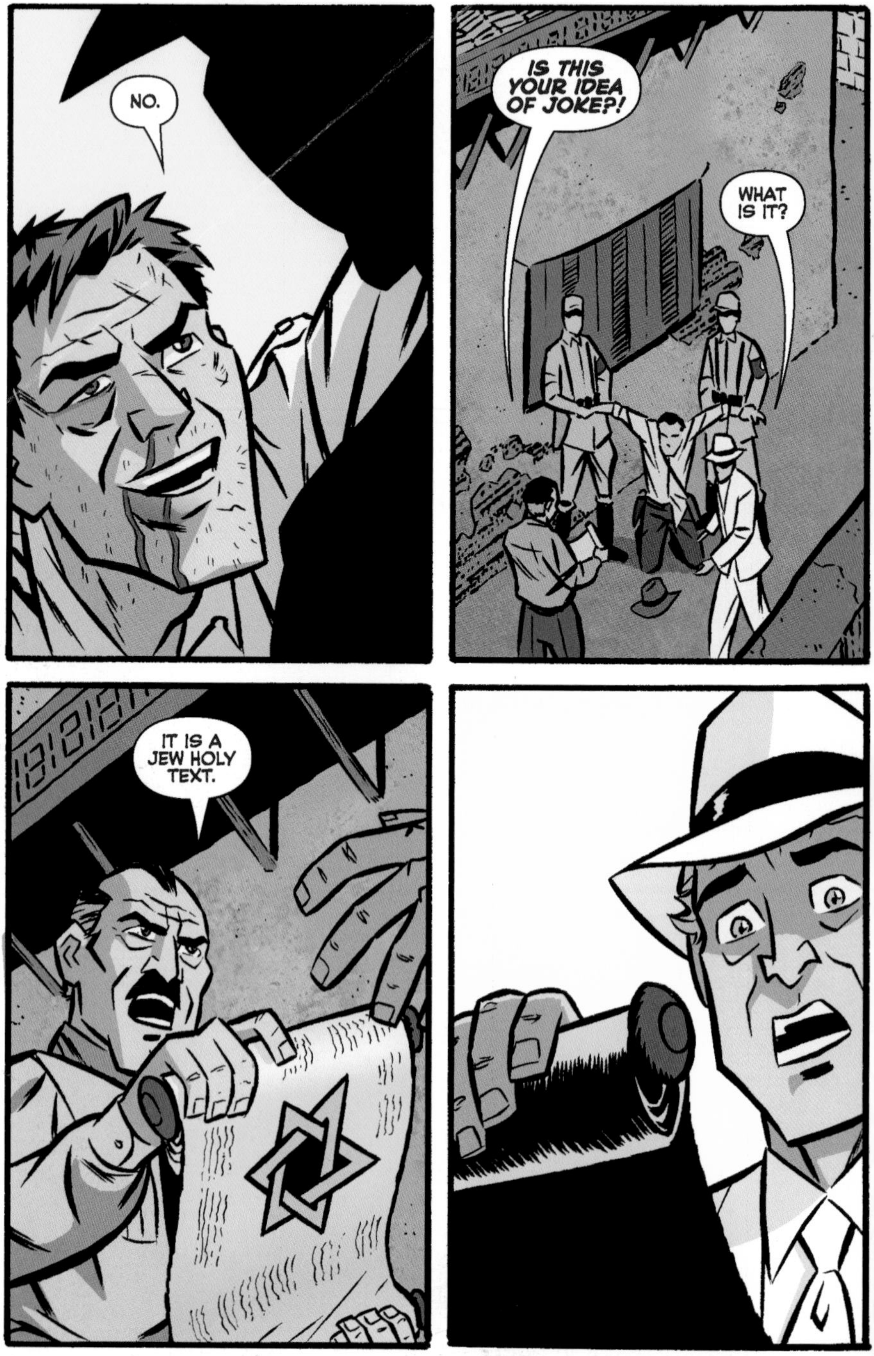
NO.
IS THIS YOUR IDEA OF JOKE?!
WHAT IS IT?
IT IS A JEW HOLY TEXT.

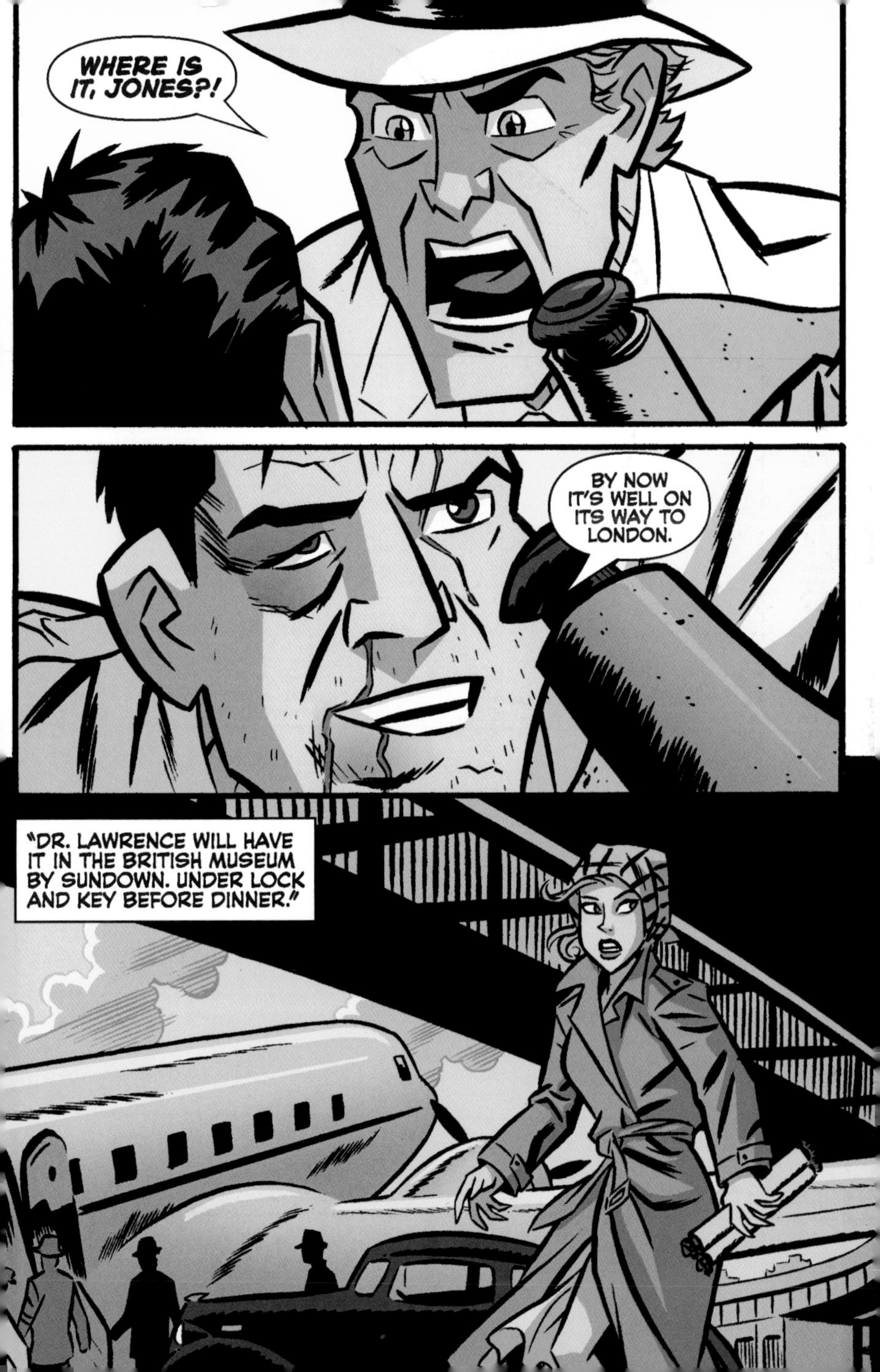
WHERE IS IT, JONES?!
BY NOW IT'S WELL ON ITS WAY TO LONDON.
"DR. LAWRENCE WILL HAVE IT IN THE BRITISH MUSEUM BY SUNDOWN. UNDER LOCK AND KEY BEFORE DINNER."

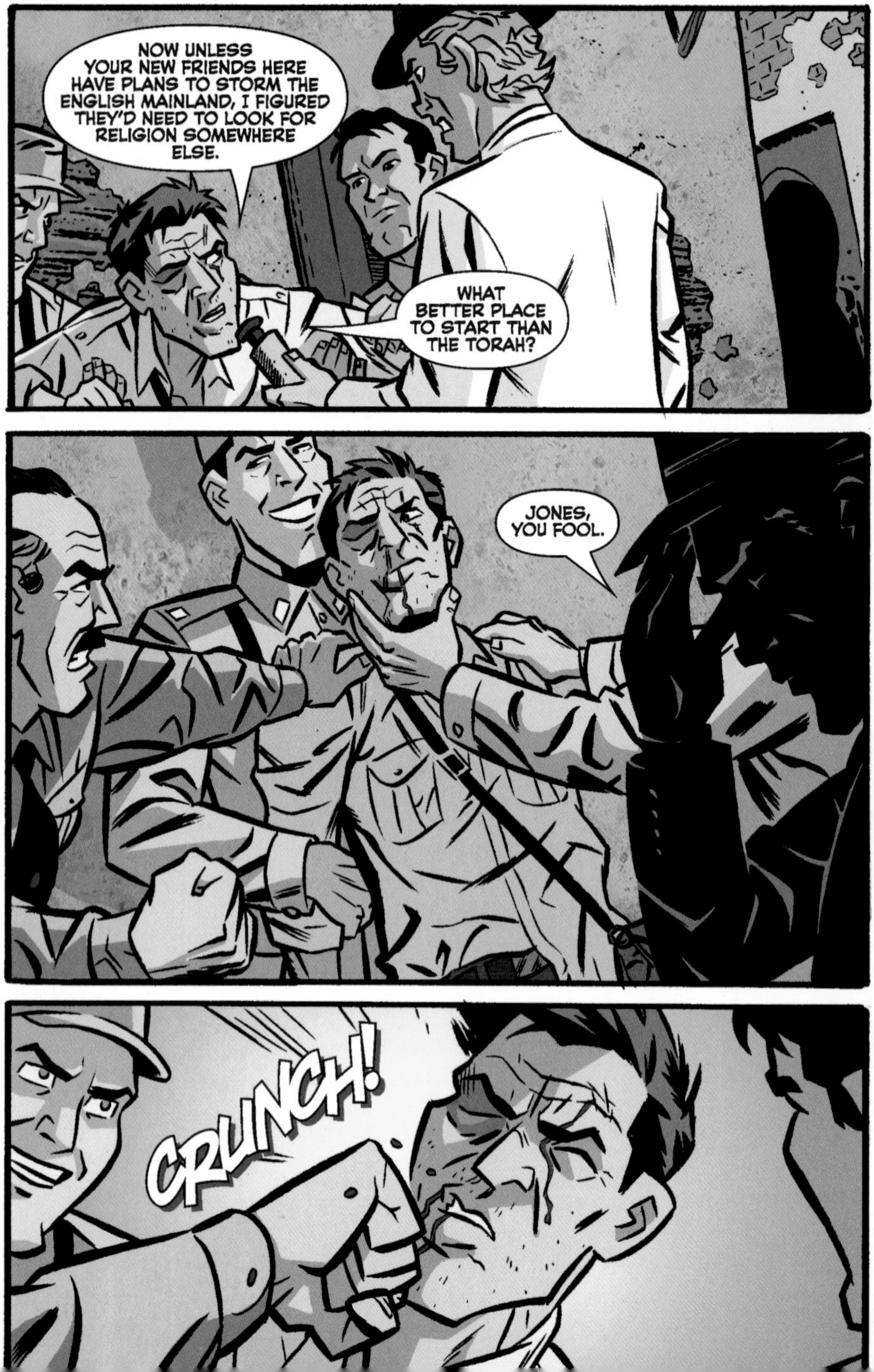
NOW UNLESS YOUR NEW FRIENDS HERE HAVE PLANS TO STORM THE ENGLISH MAINLAND, I FIGURED THEY'D NEED TO LOOK FOR RELIGION SOMEWHERE ELSE.
WHAT BETTER PLACE TO START THAN THE TORAH?
JONES, YOU FOOL.
CRUNCH!

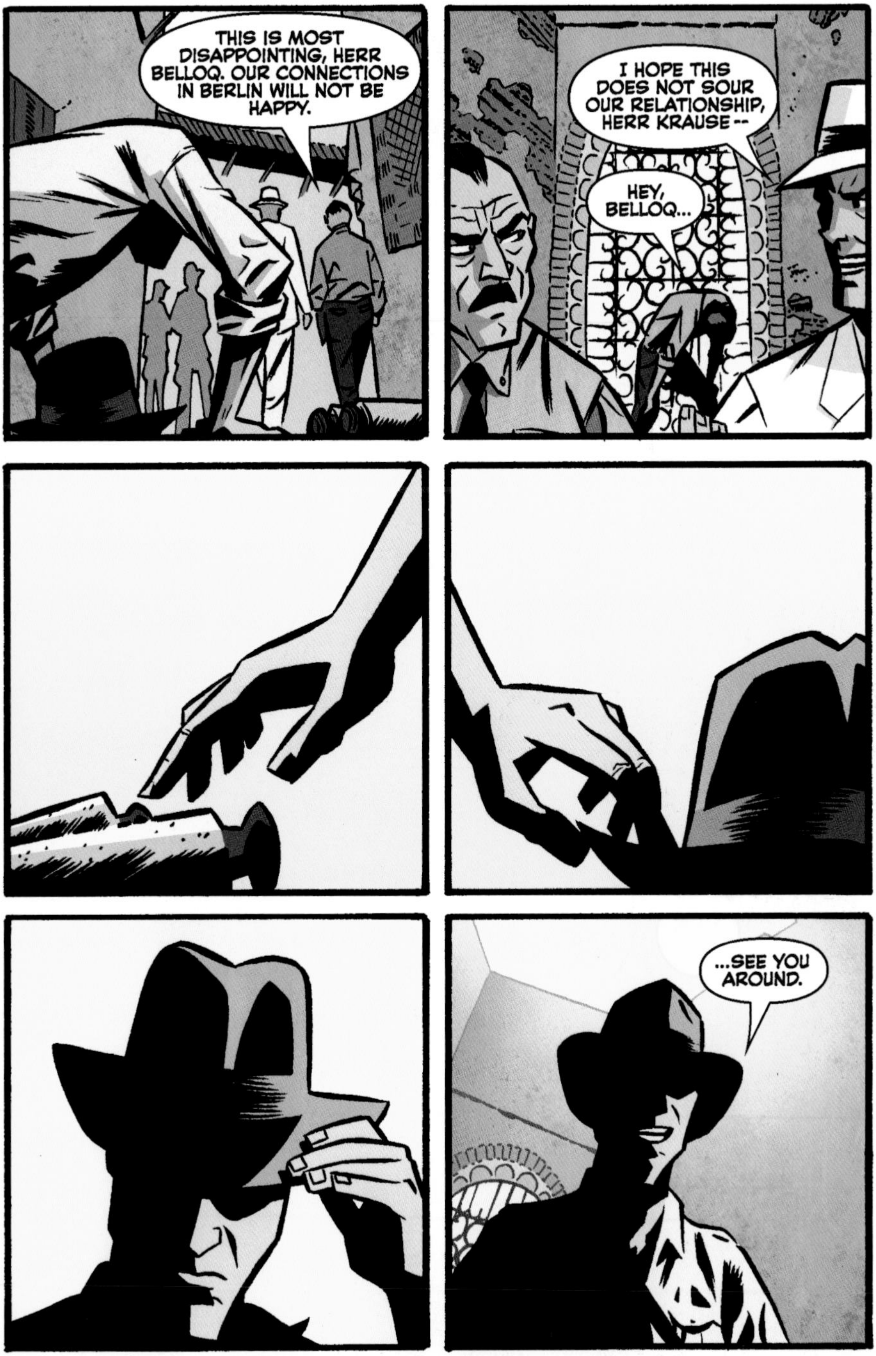
THIS IS MOST DISAPPOINTING, HERR BELLOQ. OUR CONNECTIONS IN BERLIN WILL NOT BE HAPPY.
I HOPE THIS DOES NOT SOUR OUR RELATIONSHIP, HERR KRAUSE --
HEY, BELLOQ...
...SEE YOU AROUND.

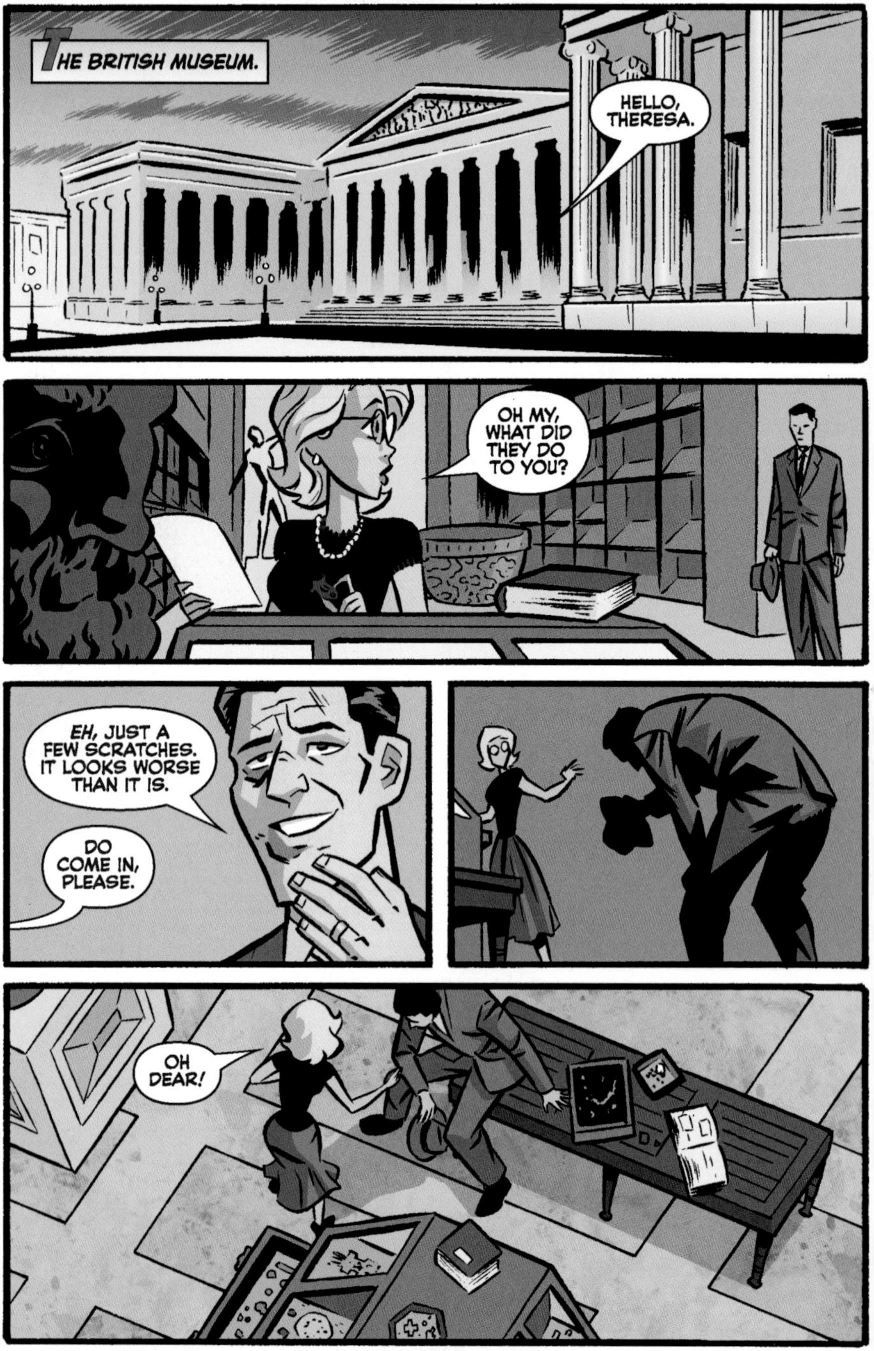
THE BRITISH MUSEUM.
HELLO, THERESA.
OH MY, WHAT DID THEY DO TO YOU?
EH, JUST A FEW SCRATCHES. IT LOOKS WORSE THAN IT IS.
DO COME IN, PLEASE.
OH DEAR!

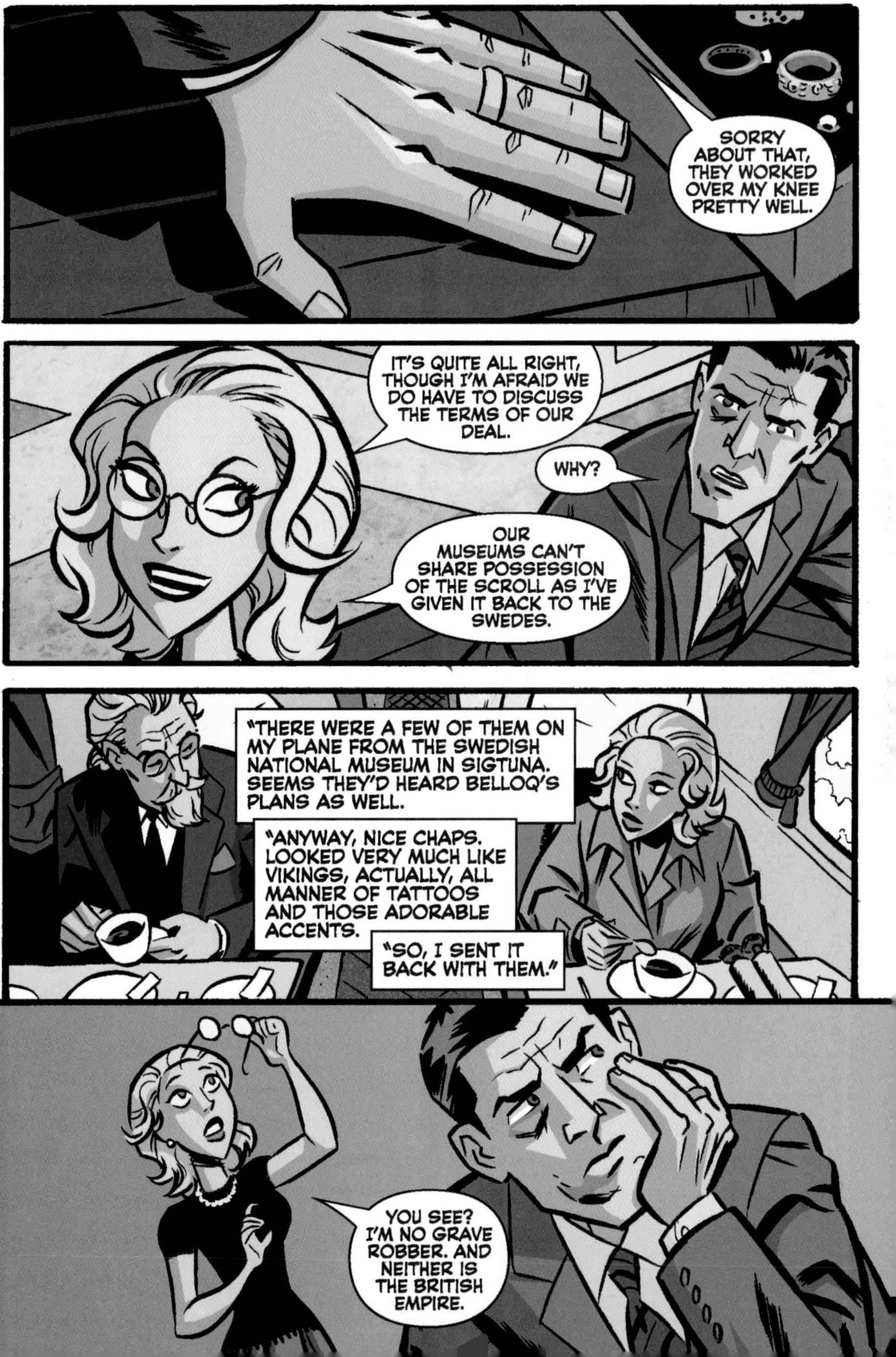
SORRY ABOUT THAT, THEY WORKED OVER MY KNEE PRETTY WELL.
IT'S QUITE ALL RIGHT, THOUGH I'M AFRAID WE DO HAVE TO DISCUSS THE TERMS OF OUR DEAL.
WHY?
OUR MUSEUMS CAN'T SHARE POSSESSION OF THE SCROLL AS I'VE GIVEN IT BACK TO THE SWEDES.
"THERE WERE A FEW OF THEM ON MY PLANE FROM THE SWEDISH NATIONAL MUSEUM IN SIGTUNA. SEEMS THEY'D HEARD BELLOQ'S PLANS AS WELL.
"ANYWAY, NICE CHAPS. LOOKED VERY MUCH LIKE VIKINGS, ACTUALLY, ALL MANNER OF TATTOOS AND THOSE ADORABLE ACCENTS.
"SO, I SENT IT BACK WITH THEM."
YOU SEE? I'M NO GRAVE ROBBER. AND NEITHER IS THE BRITISH EMPIRE.

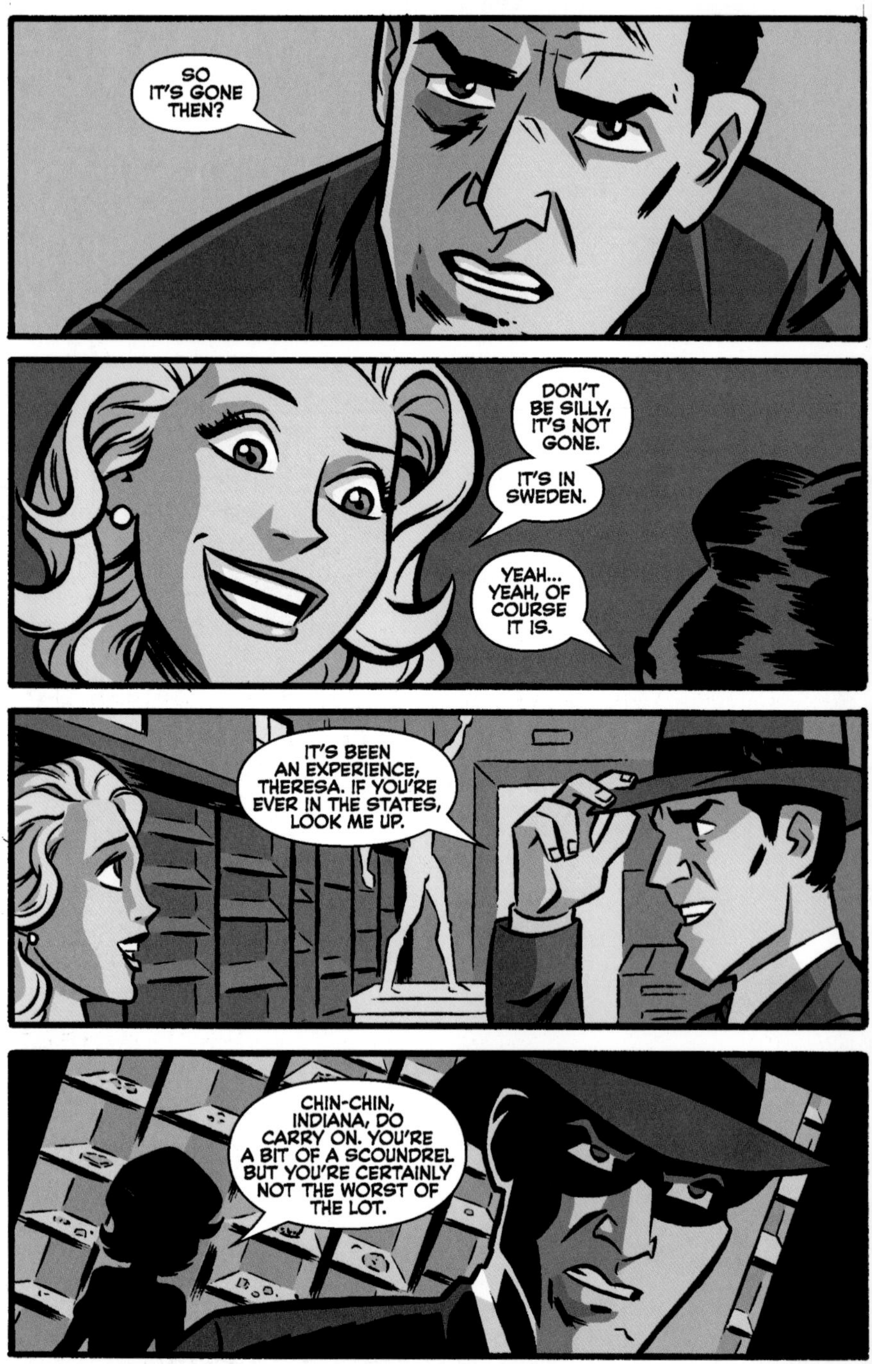
SO IT'S GONE THEN?
DON'T BE SILLY, IT'S NOT GONE.
IT'S IN SWEDEN.
YEAH... YEAH, OF COURSE IT IS.
IT'S BEEN AN EXPERIENCE, THERESA. IF YOU'RE EVER IN THE STATES, LOOK ME UP.
CHIN-CHIN, INDIANA, DO CARRY ON. YOU'RE A BIT OF A SCOUNDREL BUT YOU'RE CERTAINLY NOT THE WORST OF THE LOT.

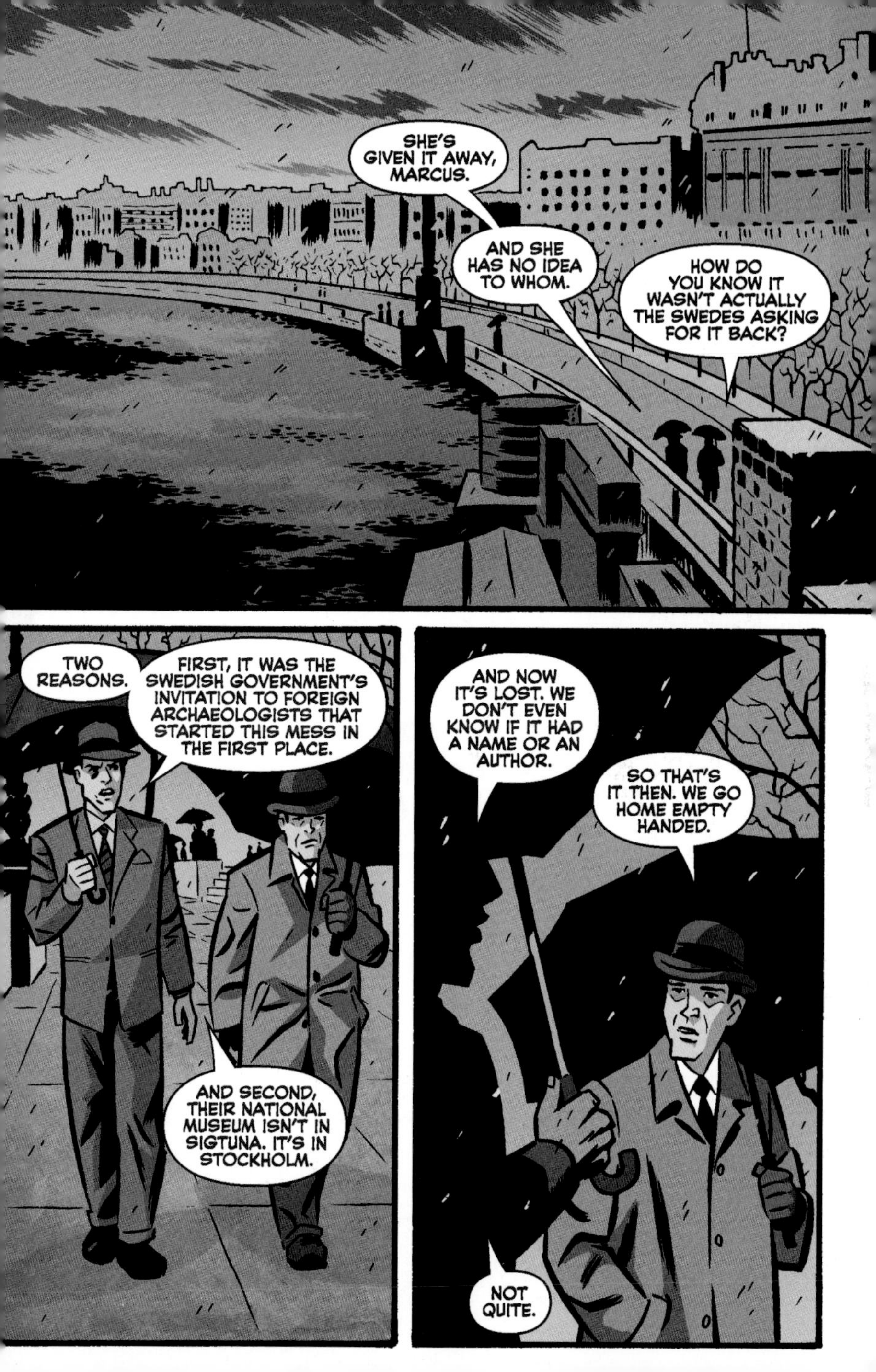
SHE'S GIVEN IT AWAY, MARCUS.
AND SHE HAS NO IDEA TO WHOM.
HOW DO YOU KNOW IT WASN'T ACTUALLY THE SWEDES ASKING FOR IT BACK?
TWO REASONS.
FIRST, IT WAS THE SWEDISH GOVERNMENT'S INVITATION TO FOREIGN ARCHAEOLOGISTS THAT STARTED THIS MESS IN THE FIRST PLACE.
AND SECOND, THEIR NATIONAL MUSEUM ISN'T IN SIGTUNA. IT'S IN STOCKHOLM.
AND NOW IT'S LOST. WE DON'T EVEN KNOW IF IT HAD A NAME OR AN AUTHOR.
SO THAT'S IT THEN. WE GO HOME EMPTY HANDED.
NOT QUITE.

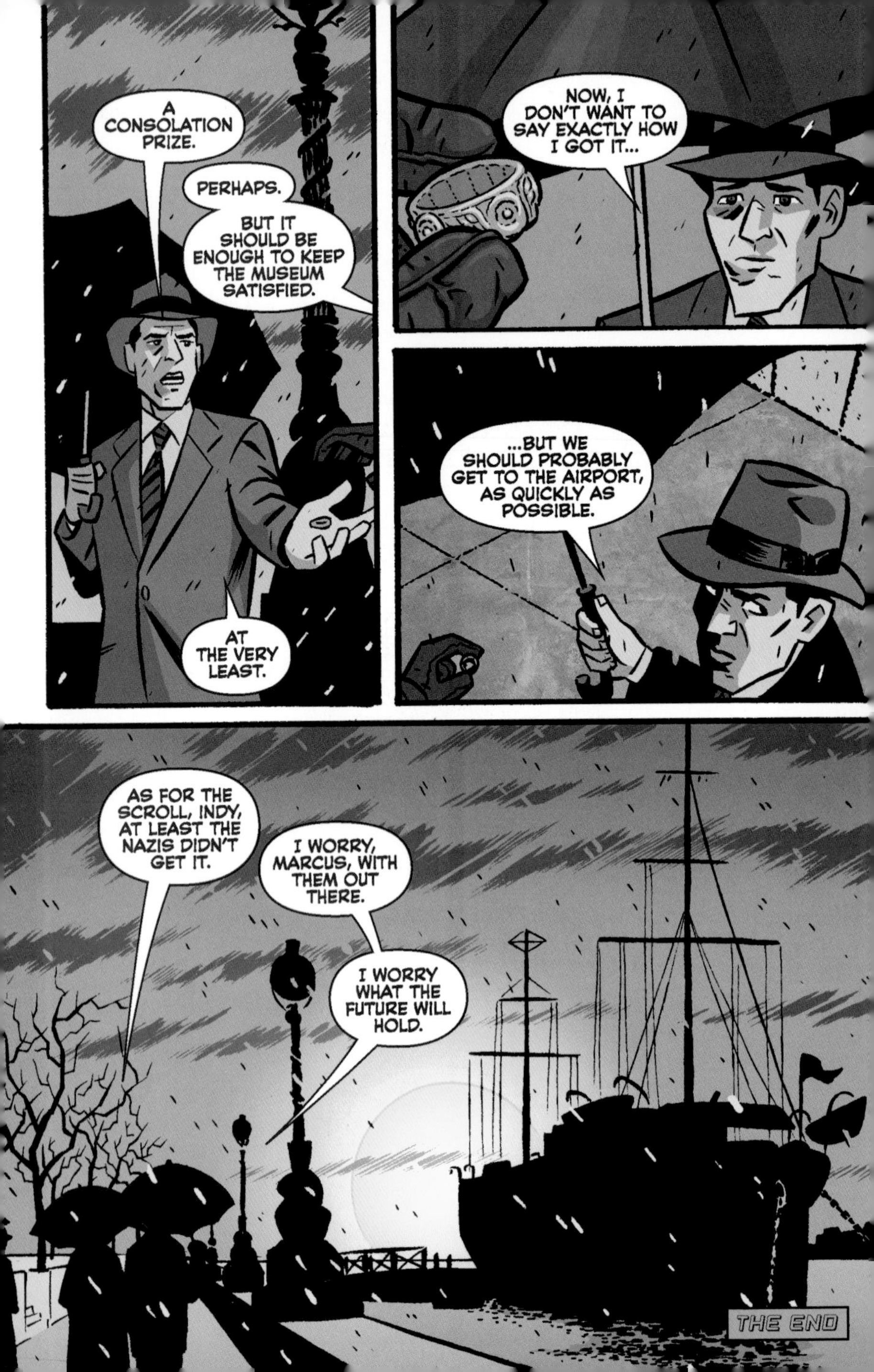
A CONSOLATION PRIZE.
PERHAPS.
BUT IT SHOULD BE ENOUGH TO KEEP THE MUSEUM SATISFIED.
AT THE VERY LEAST.
NOW, I DON'T WANT TO SAY EXACTLY HOW I GOT IT...
...BUT WE SHOULD PROBABLY GET TO THE AIRPORT, AS QUICKLY AS POSSIBLE.
AS FOR THE SCROLL, INDY, AT LEAST THE NAZIS DIDN'T GET IT.
I WORRY, MARCUS, WITH THEM OUT THERE.
I WORRY WHAT THE FUTURE WILL HOLD.
THE END

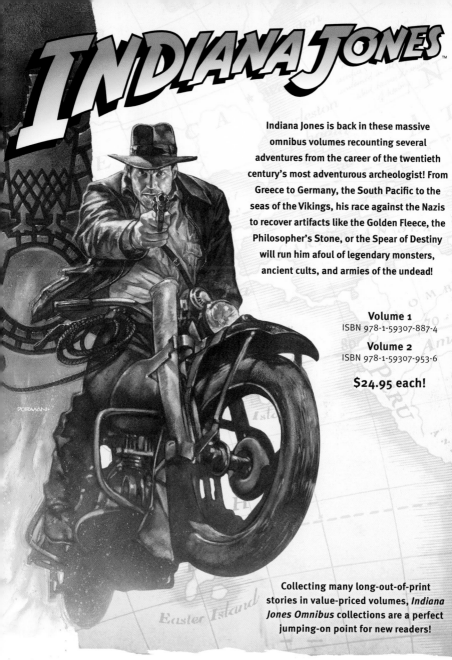

INDIANA JONES™

Indiana Jones is back in these massive omnibus volumes recounting several adventures from the career of the twentieth century's most adventurous archeologist! From Greece to Germany, the South Pacific to the seas of the Vikings, his race against the Nazis to recover artifacts like the Golden Fleece, the Philosopher's Stone, or the Spear of Destiny will run him afoul of legendary monsters, ancient cults, and armies of the undead!

Volume 1
ISBN 978-1-59307-887-4

Volume 2
ISBN 978-1-59307-953-6

$24.95 each!

Collecting many long-out-of-print stories in value-priced volumes, *Indiana Jones Omnibus* collections are a perfect jumping-on point for new readers!

READY TO TRY SOME OTHER GREAT STAR WARS® TITLES?

STAR WARS
REBELLION
Volume 1: MY BROTHER, MY ENEMY

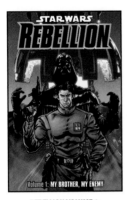

REBELLION VOLUME 1:
MY BROTHER, MY ENEMY

Imperial officer Janek "Tank" Sunber makes a critical choice between his duty to the Empire and his loyalty to childhood friend Luke Skywalker in an explosive tale of Rebel spies, Imperial ambushes, and the dreaded Darth Vader!

ISBN: 978-1-59307-711-2 | $14.95

STAR WARS
LEGACY
VOLUME 1 BROKEN

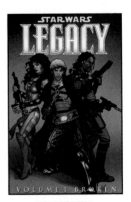

LEGACY VOLUME 1:
BROKEN

The Jedi Temple is attacked, an Emperor is betrayed, and the Sith are born anew! A lot can happen in a hundred years, but that's just the beginning of the story!

ISBN: 978-1-59307-716-7 | $17.95

STAR WARS
KNIGHTS OF THE OLD REPUBLIC
VOLUME ONE
COMMENCEMENT

KNIGHTS OF THE OLD REPUBLIC VOLUME 1:
COMMENCEMENT

Thousands of years before Luke Skywalker would destroy the Death Star in that fateful battle above Yavin 4, one lone Padawan would become a fugitive hunted by his own Masters, charged with murdering every one of his fellow Jedi-in-training!

ISBN: 978-1-59307-640-5 | $18.95

STAR WARS
DARK TIMES
Volume One: THE PATH TO NOWHERE

DARK TIMES VOLUME 1:
THE PATH TO NOWHERE

Jedi Dass Jennir and his companion Bomo Greenbark survived the Clone Wars, but the fate of Bomo's wife and daughter remains a mystery. The two friends are determined to find them, but their path leads them from danger to darkness—where each of them stands to lose more than they may hope to gain.

ISBN: 978-1-59307-792-1 | $17.95

DARK HORSE BOOKS

AVAILABLE AT YOUR LOCAL COMICS SHOP OR BOOKSTORE!

To find a comics shop in your area, call 1-888-266-4226.

For more information or to order direct visit darkhorse.com or call 1-800-862-0052 Mon.–Fri. 9 A.M. to 5 P.M. Pacific Time *Prices and availability subject to change without notice

STAR WARS®

CLONE WARS ADVENTURES

Don't miss any of the action-packed adventures of your favorite STAR WARS® characters, available at comics shops and bookstores in a galaxy near you!

STAR WARS
CLONE WARS ADVENTURES
Vol 4
STAR WARS
CLONE WARS ADVENTURES
Vol 1
THREE NEW STORIES! ALL-JEDI ACTION!
STAR WARS
CLONE WARS ADVENTURES
CLONES, DROIDS, AND BOUNTY HUNTERS IN FOUR FANTASTIC TALES!
Vol 10

$6.95 each!

Volume 1	**Volume 2**	**Volume 3**	**Volume 4**	**Volume 5**
ISBN: 978-1-59307-243-8	ISBN: 978-1-59307-271-1	ISBN: 978-1-59307-307-7	ISBN: 978-1-59307-402-9	ISBN: 978-1-59307-483-8
Volume 6	**Volume 7**	**Volume 8**	**Volume 9**	**Volume 10**
ISBN: 978-1-59307-567-5	ISBN: 978-1-59307-678-8	ISBN: 978-1-59307-680-1	ISBN: 978-1-59307-832-4	ISBN: 978-1-59307-878-2

AVAILABLE AT YOUR LOCAL COMICS SHOP OR BOOKSTORE

To find a comics shop in your area, call 1-888-266-4226

For more information or to order direct: • On the web: darkhorse.com • Phone: 1-800-862-0052 Mon.–Fri. 9 AM to 5 PM Pacific Time.
• E-mail: mailorder@darkhorse.com *Prices and availability subject to change without notice.

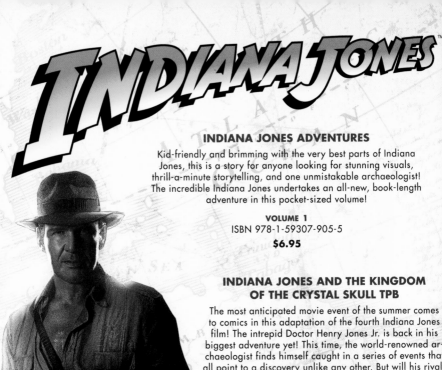

INDIANA JONES

INDIANA JONES ADVENTURES

Kid-friendly and brimming with the very best parts of Indiana Jones, this is a story for anyone looking for stunning visuals, thrill-a-minute storytelling, and one unmistakable archaeologist! The incredible Indiana Jones undertakes an all-new, book-length adventure in this pocket-sized volume!

VOLUME 1
ISBN 978-1-59307-905-5

$6.95

INDIANA JONES AND THE KINGDOM OF THE CRYSTAL SKULL TPB

The most anticipated movie event of the summer comes to comics in this adaptation of the fourth Indiana Jones film! The intrepid Doctor Henry Jones Jr. is back in his biggest adventure yet! This time, the world-renowned archaeologist finds himself caught in a series of events that all point to a discovery unlike any other. But will his rival in pursuit of this priceless treasure seize his quarry from right under his nose? Not if he, and a few unexpected companions, have anything to say about it!

ISBN 978-1-59307-952-9

$12.95

INDIANA JONES OMNIBUS

Collecting many long-out-of-print stories in value-priced volumes, *Indiana Jones Omnibus* collections are a perfect jumping-on point for new readers!

VOLUME 1
ISBN 978-1-59307-887-4

VOLUME 2
ISBN 978-1-59307-953-6

$24.95 each!